Juan and Eva Perón

SUTTON POCKET BIOGRAPHIES

Series Editor C.S. Nicholls

Highly readable brief lives of those who have played a significant part in history, and whose contributions still influence contemporary culture.

SUTTON POCKET BIOGRAPHIES

Juan and Eva Perón

CLIVE FOSS

SUTTON PUBLISHING

First published in 1999 by
Sutton Publishing Limited · Phoenix Mill
Thrupp · Stroud · Gloucestershire · GL5 2BU

British Library Cataloguing in Publication Data
A catalogue record for this book is available from the British Library

ISBN 0-7509-2104-8

Typeset in 13/18 pt Perpetua.
Typesetting and origination by
Sutton Publishing Limited.
Printed in Great Britain at
Bath Press, Bath, Avon.

CONTENTS

Chronology   vii

Introduction   xi

1   The Rise of Perón, 1895–1943   1

2   Eva Duarte, 1919–43   13

3   Gaining Power, 1943–6   25

4   The Joint Dictatorship, 1946–9   39

5   Constitution, Foundation,
       Renunciation, 1949–51   52

6   Evita's Death, Perón's
       Fall, 1951–5   66

7   Exile, 1955–73   81

8   Return and Legacy, 1973–89   98

    Notes   108

    Bibliography   110

CHRONOLOGY

1895	**8 October.** Birth of Juan Perón.
1913	Perón graduates from military academy.
1919	**7 May.** Birth of Eva Ibarguren (Duarte).
1920	Perón becomes instructor in non-commissioned officer's school.
1929	**5 January.** Perón marries Aurelia Tízon.
1930	**6 September.** Military coup; Perón participates
1931–6	Perón, professor at War Academy, writes books.
1935	**January.** Eva comes to Buenos Aires, gets her first roles on stage.
1938	**10 September.** Perón's wife dies.
1939–40	Perón posted to Italy, travels in Germany.
1939	**May.** Eva becomes heroine of soap operas; her photograph appears on magazine covers.
1943	**4 June.** Military revolution which Perón helped plan.
	27 November. Perón becomes Secretary of Labour and Welfare.
1944	**22 January.** Benefit for San Juan earthquake; Perón meets Evita.
1945	**9 October.** Perón forced out of all his posts.
	17 October. Huge workers' demonstration brings back Perón.
	22 October. Perón marries Eva.

Chronology

1946	**24 February.** Perón elected President.
	4 June. Perón takes office.
	17 June. Perón creates Sole Party of the Revolution.
	25 July 1949. The party becomes Peronist Party.
1947	**6 June–23 August.** Eva's Rainbow Tour of Europe.
1948	**8 July.** Eva Maria Duarte de Perón Social Aid Foundation established; name changed to Eva Perón Foundation in 1949.
1949	**16 March.** New Constitution comes into effect.
	30 July. Eva founds Women's Peronist Party.
1951	**26 January.** Perón closes last independent paper, *La Prensa*.
	22 August. Public meeting demands Eva as Vice-President.
	31 August. She declines offer.
	6 November. Eva operated on for cancer.
1952	**4 June.** Perón inaugurated for second term; Eva's last public appearance.
	26 July. Death of Eva.
1954	**17 October.** Perón begins to attack the Catholic church.
1955	**16 June.** Navy revolt bombs Buenos Aires; mobs burn cathedral.
	16–20 September. 'Liberating Revolution' deposes Perón.
	December. Perón meets Isabel Martínez in Panama.
1957	Eva's body buried in Italy early in the year.

Chronology

1960   **January.** Perón settles in Spain, where he stays for thirteen years.

1961   **November.** Perón marries Isabel.

1966   **May.** Isabel brings López Rega to Spain; he gains influence over Perón.

1971   **2 September.** Eva's body exhumed and delivered to Perón.

1973   **25 May.** Perón's man Cámpora inaugurated as President.

1973   **20 June.** Perón returns to Argentina.
          23 September. Perón elected President for third term, with Isabel as Vice-President.

1974   **1 July.** Death of Perón.

1976   **22 October.** Eva buried in Buenos Aires' Recoleta cemetery.

INTRODUCTION

Even before Madonna, the musical *Evita* revived public interest in one of the most remarkable women of modern times. A generation after her death in 1952 at the age of thirty-three, she was a romantic legend, but her life was no less incredible. Born in rural poverty, she acted on the stage and radio, married the president of a rich and powerful country and became the most famous woman in the world. Eva Perón's impassioned devotion to social welfare earned her the love of the common people, while her ambition and vindictiveness made most others hate her. Some considered her a whore; others wanted her canonized. Consequently, it is hard to achieve an objective view of her career. Nor can she be separated from her husband, who was ultimately responsible for her success and fame.

Juan Perón towers like an unwelcome Titan over the recent history of Argentina. Many revile the memory of the populist dictator who for thirty years dominated the country from the army, the presidential palace or exile, and whose presence is still felt. But others admire his sympathy with the working class and his transformation of Argentine political life. Perón was a man of contradictions: a dictator who crushed civil liberties yet gave new rights to urban and rural workers; an army officer who became the hero of labour; a teacher who disdained the truth; a polite and charming colleague who could never be trusted.

Perón was an army officer from 1913 until 1955. More a professor of military history than a fighter, he learned the ways of intrigue well enough to help found a secret organization within the army that seized power in 1943. He was the strong man of the military regime when he met the famous actress Eva Duarte. He married her after a temporary fall from power, then went on to become freely elected president in 1946.

Juan and Eva Perón formed an unbeatable team. He ran the government while she took care of the people. Her enormously rich Foundation provided social welfare on a scale unknown before and generated a tremendous devotion that is still real. Her early death was a catastrophe for the poor, and for Perón. After it, his behaviour became increasingly erratic until a coup finally removed him in 1955. For most dictators, losing office is permanent if not fatal, but Perón never gave up, nor did the workers abandon him. During eighteen years of exile, he constantly encouraged his followers and destabilized the country. Finally, an old man with only a few months left, he returned in 1973, for a last brief and inglorious term as president.

This joint biography seeks to present these two lives as they were intertwined, following the fortunes of both together against the background of Argentina. It is intended as a basic introduction, not a history of the period, which can be found in the more comprehensive works in the bibliography.

I am especially grateful to Maximo and Elisa Gainza Paz, who guided me through the intricacies of Argentine society and history, and introduced me to many helpful friends, notably Hernán Milberg, Benito Llambí, Arthur Edbrooke, Dr Eduardo Roca and their Peronist maid Rosa. This work is not long enough to include all I learned from them or from Lucas Christeller of Lobos and his family. Mariano Plotkin gave some useful references, the librarians and archivists of the Hoover Institution facilitated research, and Tim Markey and William MacDonald read parts of the manuscript. My thanks to all.

THE RISE OF PERÓN, 1895–1943

The vast fertile plains that give Argentina its wealth encircle the town of Lobos, about 60 miles from Buenos Aires, where Juan Domingo Perón was born on 8 October 1895. He spent his first four years in an undistinguished house, neither rich nor poor, at the edge of the town where his father managed an estate. A hundred years later, the house, which has a couple of small rooms on the street and several more arranged along the inner courtyard, contained a small museum, but no original furniture, for it had been sacked during a previous regime. The house, like the country, flourished or suffered from the violent feelings roused by the man born in it.

Perón's father, Mario Tomás, was a drifter who never made a success of life. He began by studying medicine, after the example of his own father, Tomás Liberato Perón, a distinguished doctor honoured by the state. The family's origin is unclear: when Perón became famous, he would tell Spaniards that the family originated in Sardinia, and Italians that the Peronis or Perrons were from northern Italy. Mario Tomás abandoned medicine for the life of a rancher, settling first in Lobos where he met Juana Sosa Toledo, a part-Indian woman who bore him two sons: Mario in 1891 and Juan four years later. Eventually, in 1901, he married her: Juan Domingo never seemed bothered by the fact that he was illegitimate. By that time, the family had moved on to the bleak and frigid plains of Patagonia, then to a somewhat milder region closer to the centre of the country. Through many moves and disappointments, Juana was the mainstay of the family. Perón admired her strong will and immense practical skills, but his relationship with his dignified and austere father was more distant.

Juan Domingo grew up in the open country, riding, hunting and sharing the life of ranchers, shepherds and farmhands. He developed a special and lasting affection for the unassuming local people. The long winter nights left time for reading his father's books on religion, philosophy and science. Formal education started at the age of nine, when he was sent away to the capital to study and live with his aunts. He adapted to school in this more complex and disciplined world, but missed the free life of the country.

Sports appealed more to Perón than his studies. Juan Domingo persevered in medicine as his father wished, though his real love was engineering. When he was fifteen, however, some friends persuaded him to join them in taking the examination for admission to the national military academy. He passed, entered, completed the three-year course in two years and graduated as a second lieutenant in 1913. Discipline and a superb memory ensured success in what became his path in life.

The Argentine army, large and underemployed, had not fought a war for sixty years and faced no immediate threats. Traditionally, its officers had been from the land-owning aristocracy and its enlisted men peasants or immigrants, but now a promising cadet could rise regardless of social origin. The army had long admired German military efficiency. Officers studied in Germany and Germans came to Argentina to give advice and training. Argentine officers imitated the German style, even to the heavy capes and spiked helmets that were still fashionable in 1930.

Perón joined the unaristocratic infantry, and was sent to a depressed region in the north-east, where he came into contact with rural poverty. He also learned about labour when his unit was sent to suppress a strike in 1919. He later claimed that his discussions with the strike leaders inspired his lifelong sympathy for organized labour. The following year he became an instructor in the school for non-commissioned officers at the vast Campo de Mayo garrison outside the capital. Perón's enthusiasm for sport helped him develop a real rapport with his men. He became fencing champion of the army, was an excellent boxer and introduced new sports and better training into the curriculum. He especially liked to challenge his best men in track and boxing; since he was stronger and taller than most, he usually won. He treated his men with a real respect and affection, very different from the distant formality of his colleagues. He gained their loyalty by speaking with them simply and directly, and helping them with their personal problems, but he always maintained his own dignity and a certain reserve. Throughout his life, Perón was congenial and persuasive, people enjoyed his company, he seemed calm and good tempered, but he never became a close friend or shared his private life.

A natural leader with an immense capacity for physical or mental work, Perón also showed a powerful didactic streak. He loved to lecture and to write articles, books and manuals – the beginning of a long career of instructing the public. In 1926, his superiors recognized his abilities by sending him to the War Academy, the gate to high promotion. After completing the three-year course, he was assigned to the General Staff in Buenos Aires, the most desirable posting in the army, where a man of ambition would be in contact with the highest officers.

By 1930, Captain Perón had become a leader, but an infantry commander in a peacetime army in a country with a long tradition of civilian rule had no opportunity to lead. Instead, he turned to more pacific and domestic pursuits. His position allowed him the leisure time to embark on serious research in military history, and he married a respectable young teacher from the capital, Aurelia Tizón. She played the piano and helped him with his work, and he shared the cooking with her, especially when there was company. His life seemed completely tranquil when Revolution set Perón and Argentina on a new course.

While Perón was growing up, Argentina was enjoying a golden age of tremendous prosperity and political calm. Its vast production of meat and grain, mostly exported to Europe, guaranteed a large income to the owners of the land, an aristocracy of some 200 families which came to be called the Oligarchy. They controlled the government and were closely allied to the British who owned the railways and most of the public utilities. Argentina was a republic modelled on the United States, but its president had a special power that allowed him to 'intervene' or seize control of any province. The country was not a democracy, for the Oligarchy made sure that its own men held the highest offices. This system offered stability until 1916, when the Radical Yrigoyen took power. Enormous popularity allowed him to make reforms, but in his second term he became senile, his followers were notoriously corrupt and the political system was paralysed. The great Depression compounded the crisis by reducing exports and causing an influx of the rural poor to slums around the capital.

The situation demanded and produced a drastic solution. On 6 September 1930, General José Felix Uriburu took control. He wanted to restore order under a military government, expel the politicians and create a corporate state based on the model of Mussolini's Italy. Instead, his support in the army proved too narrow to promote such changes, and he agreed to elections in 1932. They returned the Anglophile General Agustín Justo and introduced the so-called Infamous Decade, when notoriously crooked elections allowed an oligarchic regime, backed by a powerful military faction, to stay in power.

The revolution of 1930 included Captain Juan Perón, who published a memoir about it a year later. He relates that he was approached secretly by fellow officers, met the leaders and was surprised to find how few they actually were. Since he agreed with the ideology, he joined them, despite misgivings about the planning. The future dictator drew important lessons from the events: that plots needed to be carefully organized with widespread backing in the army and, most importantly, among the general population. Uriburu's coup succeeded almost by a miracle: his small force could easily have been stopped had not the public helped to occupy the government palace and obstruct loyalist units. Perón saw such mass political action as the wave of the future.

Perón eventually returned to his old job as professor of military history. He threw himself into it, producing three large works in five years. These textbooks on the First World War (1932), military history (1933) and the Russo-Japanese War (1933–4) offered clear analytical accounts of battles, tactics and strategy and show the influence of German military theories. They were the unoriginal products of diligent research, intended as textbooks for the Academy, where Perón was a conscientious teacher. Surviving examination papers with corrections in his hand are filled with careful and detailed criticism, usually tempered with words of encouragement.

In 1936, he received his first foreign posting, as military attaché in Chile. Contrary to later rumours, he was not expelled for spying (which, after all, was his job), but did leave a system of espionage that caused great embarrassment for his successor, Major Eduardo Lonardi. Perón returned to the capital, where he suffered a devastating blow: his wife, who was not yet thirty, died of cancer of the uterus in September 1938; they had no children. Perón was consoling himself with teaching, writing and organizing athletics for poor children when his life took another turn.

In February 1939, he was posted to Italy to work with Alpine troops, a natural assignment for such an avid sportsman. During his two-year stay, which coincided with the outbreak of the Second World War, Perón came to know and admire Fascist Italy and Germany. The military efficiency of the Axis and its ability to mobilize a whole population for war made a deep impression. So did Mussolini's skill at rousing huge crowds and the social reforms he espoused. Perón was in the throng when the Duce declared war, though he did not have the private interview that he later advertised. For Perón, the truth, especially about himself, was of no importance. His European sojourn strengthened the view he shared with many of his colleagues, that the Axis would win the war.

Back in Argentina at the end of 1940, Perón was assigned to a division of mountain troops in Mendoza at the base of the Andes. His commander was General Edelmiro Farrell, who had also been trained in Italy. One of his colleagues was Colonel Domingo Mercante. These were momentous associations: Farrell became Perón's patron and constant supporter; Mercante his closest associate. In March 1942, Farrell brought Perón to the capital, where the deeply divided army was plunged in intrigue.

By now, Argentina had recovered from the Depression and entered once again into great prosperity. Justo built massive public works, notably the widest street in the world, the Ninth of July Avenue that cuts a block-wide swathe a mile through the heart of the capital, suitable for titanic mass demonstrations. Trade and industry grew, creating a class of entrepreneurs with no place in the traditional political structure, and an industrial proletariat that impelled the growth of trade unions. The government was closely allied with Great Britain, but many others, hostile to British economic domination, listened to the appealing propaganda from Italy and Germany. The Second World War intensified these divisions. Although Argentina remained neutral, the army, which had a powerful pro-Axis faction, constantly plotted against the politicians, who, it suspected, would surrender to Allied pressure and abandon neutrality.

The heart of conspiracy was a secret organization, the GOU or Unification Group, the Grupo Obra de Unificación. This uninformative name concealed a revolutionary network. The seed of the GOU was planted, apparently by Perón, in 1942, with the backing of General Farrell. Its principles were vague and uncontroversial, stressing unity, honour and loyalty. Officers pledged to resist outside influences (especially from the United States) and internal instability, such as a Communist-led popular front. Most importantly, they were to defend neutrality, the symbol of Argentine independence. The ideals were highly nationalistic, without being specifically pro-Axis. The GOU was a secret organization based on small cells whose members knew only one another. No civilians were admitted, the membership was anonymous and loyalty was ensured by signed undated letters of resignation. A central body of nineteen officers co-ordinated activities. Its directors were Perón, who became secretary to the Minister of War, the chief of police, the President's secretary and the head of army intelligence. Others occupied similarly vital positions in the army and government.

Although they plotted constantly, the officers were almost overtaken by events. When the President announced that a notoriously corrupt crony would be his successor and seemed about to abandon neutrality, the GOU decided to move. It co-opted a respected general, Arturo Rawson, to lead the march on the presidential palace. The military took over and proclaimed the revolution on 4 June 1943. After the coup, the GOU pledged its allegiance to the new government, and vowed to fight corruption, purge the political system and reduce the influence of the rich. When they realized, however, that Rawson actually favoured the Allies and proposed bringing civilians into the government, they threw him out. He had only lasted two days. General Pedro Ramirez, a GOU man, became President, with General Farrell as his Minister of War. Farrell's secretary was Perón, who became the dominant figure of the regime by using methods that few of his colleagues could even imagine.

EVA DUARTE,
1919–43

W hen Eva Perón was famous, people loved or hated her with equal abandon. As a result, her early life and career are portrayed in the blackest terms or in uninformative blandness. Virtually every statement has an alternative version, often just as convincing. Yet it is still possible to reconstruct an image of an obscure child of rural poverty rising to become the most famous woman in the world.

Eva Maria Ibarguren was born on 7 May 1919 in the dusty hamlet of Los Toldos, in the midst of the endless plains 150 miles west of Buenos Aires. Her father, Juan Duarte, was a moderately successful landowner and local political boss who employed Eva's mother, Juana Ibarguren, as cook. She was also his mistress of long standing, presenting him with five children of whom Eva was the youngest. Juana and her children lived not on the ranch, but in a small house on the main street of the town; Duarte's actual wife stayed in Chivilcoy, 20 miles away. But the appearance of propriety, strengthened by the family's appropriation of the name Duarte, could never remove the stigma of illegitimacy.

In 1920, when Eva was still a baby, Duarte returned to live with his wife. Juana moved to a smaller house in a less desirable neighbourhood, and took up sewing. A diploma in dressmaking from the local school gave a qualification, and incessant hard work enabled her to raise her brood. Toys were scarce and second-hand, and poverty was never far away, but Juana kept the children clean and well dressed. She worked so hard that she developed varicose veins and had to be helped to the sewing machine, but she never abandoned her pretensions to respectability. Nor did the small Eva ever forget the sewing machine.

In 1926, when Eva was seven, Juan Duarte was killed in an automobile accident. Juana appeared at the funeral with her children, unacceptable behaviour for a mistress, who had no place at such a solemn family occasion. Duarte's wife refused to let them in, but an uncle relented and allowed the children a brief glimpse of the body and then to follow behind the funeral procession. Eva had already learned from the stares or silence of other children that illegitimacy was no desirable state, but the funeral burned an indelible impression into her soul.

Duarte had got a job for Elisa, the eldest sister, in the local post office, patronage that helped support the family. In 1929, though, a new local administration fired her. With the mayor's help, Juana managed to find Elisa a post in Junín, a much larger town, and so the family embarked on a new life there in 1930. The second sister, Blanca, became a teacher and the only brother, Juan, found work as a soap salesman. With brighter economic prospects, Juana left sewing behind and began keeping a boarding house. Passing herself off as a respectable widow, she attracted a serious clientele which came to include the principal of a local college, an army major and a lawyer.

By now, Eva had developed into a thin, dark-eyed, dreamy and solemn girl who threw occasional tantrums. She never seems to be smiling in early family photographs. Her record in school was mediocre but she excelled in poetry, for which she had an excellent memory, though her diction was poor. On rainy days, when discipline was lax and many children stayed away, Eva would go from class to class reciting 'poetries' as she called them. Her favourite recreation, though, was the cinema. On Sundays, the girls would promenade around the main square eating ice creams and pretending to ignore the rude comments of the boys, for they could only afford the films on Tuesdays, when a cheap matinee, usually with two or three features, allowed them to escape into a fabulous dream world. Eva especially adored Norma Shearer, who had risen from poverty to star as the supremely glamorous Marie Antoinette. She read about her and the other stars in movie magazines like *Sintonia* and collected her photographs. Soon, Eva determined to become an actress herself.

Eva had her stage debut at the age of fourteen, when she obtained a small part in a school play. She also recited poetry at a microphone in front of the local music store, but there was only one place that offered any real possibilities, the fabulous Buenos Aires, a vast cosmopolitan, sophisticated city, the largest and richest in South America. Her arrival there is deeply shrouded in mythology. The most popular version associates it with the famous tango singer Agustín Magaldi. She supposedly appeared in his dressing room after a performance in Junín, seduced him and went off to the capital in his railway compartment. Alternatively, her brother Juan got her an introduction to Magaldi, who helped her after her arrival. Actually, there is no evidence that Magaldi was ever in Junín in 1934 and no reason to believe that such a good family man would have been inflamed by a skinny fifteen-year-old girl. Other stories associate her with another singer. More prosaic, and perhaps more plausible, is the version that says she was accompanied by her mother, who installed her in a boarding house near the Congress run by a friend from Junín. In any case, Eva left the provinces behind forever in January 1935.

Wealth and glitter dominated the capital that was emerging from the Depression, yet poverty was never far away from immigrants like Eva who were flocking in from the countryside. Justo's government was creating new jobs in industry, but the competition was intense and the general mood, reflected in the popular tango, was melancholy, sardonic and often bitter. A raw country girl like Eva, with no powerful connections, no experience and limited talents, could only face a long struggle. She was fortunate to have a base in the boarding house whose manager often overlooked her late or missing rent. Within three months, she managed to get a small role in a comedy, then a few others during the rest of the year. None lasted long, but all demanded constant performance, often seven days a week. These were marginal, irregular jobs; actresses, especially minor ones, were poorly paid, if at all, and had no security. If the play flopped, the cast would be back on the street, looking for new roles.

In 1936, Eva toured with the company of José Franco, who introduced her to a reality of the profession: he told her to sleep with him or find her own way back from Mendoza, at the base of the Andes. Eva stayed with the company. Later in the year, an obese but highly successful critic and director, Pablo Suero, 'the Toad', gave her a role in a play by Lillian Hellman, which even took her to Montevideo. On her return, she went to the crowded theatre where the Toad was working, looking for a new role. He told her in a loud voice, in public, that the fact that he had slept with her meant nothing and that he had no work for her. She blanched, bit her lip and walked off. Humiliation was no stranger to her.

By this time, Eva was beginning to attract attention. A fellow actress remembered her as 'young and very pretty, with dark eyes, deep red lips and skin the color and texture of a magnolia; she seemed a personification of innocence';[1] she was then seventeen. Innocent was not a word normally applied to actresses. In fact, they were so poorly paid that most of them necessarily had gentlemen who maintained them for varying periods. Reality is elusive: Eva probably succumbed to the casting couch, like other actresses, and no doubt had men friends, but she certainly was not yet profiting from them, for she lived simply and never seemed to have enough to eat. Her first encounter with the aristocracy also does not suggest licentiousness: when she was sixteen, she and a girl friend were taken to the seaside resort Mar del Plata by two rich young men who tried to seduce them, then threw them out naked when they resisted. There is nothing to suggest that Eva was especially promiscuous, but her known affairs do seem to have had a practical goal.

In 1937, Eva got her first bit part in a film and her first role in radio. Real opportunity came the following March, when she entered a radio contest organized by the same *Sintonia* magazine she had read as a young girl. The editor, a dashing ex-racing-car driver Emilio Kartulowicz, took a fancy to her and soon became her protector, promoter and lover. He even published her picture in his magazine. For Eva, it may have been romance, but Kartulowicz soon wearied of the clinging persistence that led her to wait endless hours outside his office or to follow him when he was trying to escape to the country with another woman. Soon after, Eva, who was still primarily a stage actress, got a part in the company of the well-known Pierina Dealessi, who took pity on her and became a real friend. She described Eva, then nineteen, as pale, thin and sad with hands cold and clammy from hunger, a girl who never seemed to eat and came early to the theatre because it was warmer than her room. Misery and the stage were soon to end, though, as Eva broke through into stardom.

Years later, Eva told her confessor, Father Benitez, 'In the theatre, I was awful; in movies, I managed; but if I was good at something, it was radio.'[2] In 1939, she found her real métier, as the heroine of the enormously popular soap operas that women all over the country followed avidly. Her high-pitched voice, which excelled at conveying suffering, and her rough diction were suited to the romantic 'Cinderella' roles that brought her fame. She appeared on the cover of radio magazines and was featured in their gossipy stories. By now, she had given up the stage, but continued to get minor roles in films and to do modelling: her strong features and mass of curled upswept hair were suited to displaying the flounced dresses and elaborate hats of the day.

As she became better known, she attracted fans of all kinds. She met and charmed writers, producers and rich sponsors, who could all help her career. In 1941 and 1942, her picture appeared more frequently in radio and film magazines, and a rich soap manufacturer sponsored her own programme, which meant a regular income for the first time. Finally, she could leave the boarding house and move to Posadas Street near the radio station, in the most elegant district of the capital. Some claimed that the apartment actually belonged to Colonel Imbert, a rising figure in the GOU who had taken Eva on as his mistress. In fact, she did not meet the colonel until 1943, but rumours grew together with her fame. This period is the origin of the myth of Eva the Whore, a reputation that would never leave her. She was portrayed as frequenting cafés and nightclubs where she met useful men, exploited them during a short liaison, then discarded them for more important lovers. Cash from such friends, whether earned in a night or over a period, supposedly enabled her to save her brother Juan when he was caught embezzling money from the bank where he worked. There is no way to judge these stories: actresses were regarded as not very different from prostitutes, and many of them certainly did use men to help their finances and careers. Eva would have been remarkable if she had not. In any case, she had by now acquired the hard, professional and flashy look of fame.

When the military took over in 1943, Eva was already a star. She had security in a contract with Radio Belgrano, but the new regime threatened major changes. One of its first decrees regulated the media and demanded that radio and screen have a moral and nationalistic content; all scripts were to be submitted to military censors and actors would need permits to perform. When Eva was called in, she was delighted to discover Oscar Nicolini, an old friend of her mother's from Junín, sitting beside the censor. He approved her suggestion for a programme, *My Kingdom for Love*, that would present heroines of history in an edifying light. So did his boss, the Minister of Posts, Colonel Imbert.

Eva's career now rose to new heights. Her salary increased and in August she became one of the founders of the Argentine Radio Association, a government-sponsored performers' union. Her new programme, to begin at the end of the year, was announced in *Antena* magazine as featuring the famous star Eva Duarte. Success brought new and important contacts. Through Nicolini, and Imbert, she became well acquainted with the military whose favour was overwhelmingly important. Her path soon crossed that of a well-known widower, the colonel widely believed to be the power behind the regime, Juan Perón.

There are many versions of the historic meeting between the actress and the colonel. The most colourful invokes the earthquake that destroyed the city of San Juan in January 1944. Perón organized a benefit gala featuring stars of film and radio on 22 January. The famous film actress Libertad Lamarque was seated on the stage next to Colonel Perón. When she got up to make some remarks, Eva grabbed her seat and talked incessantly and so successfully that Perón remained with her the whole evening, the next night and the rest of her life. Others give different details, most associated with the same occasion, but none so dramatic. Equally likely, she met him at a party at the radio station in October 1943, or when he organized relief by having well-known actresses collect funds on the main shopping street.

Soon after their meeting, Perón disposed of the teenage girlfriend he had introduced in public as his daughter, and moved into an apartment next to Eva's. He visited the radio studio and allowed himself to be photographed with Eva, who openly became his mistress. Their lives were irrevocably linked.

THREE

GAINING POWER,
1943–6

The new regime moved fast. Within hours of the Revolution, it ordered censorship of the press; elections were postponed; and in July it moved against Labour. Communist unions were closed down and the rest put under military administration; refractory labour leaders went to the new concentration camps in Patagonia. In August, all adult males were required to register with the police and to carry identification documents. Schoolbooks were required to praise the fatherland and the military, and in October the universities were closed after a student strike. They soon reopened, without the student federations and the many purged professors. The year ended with a sweeping decree that banned all political parties; made religious education compulsory in the schools; and dealt firmly with the media. All publishers and journalists had to register with the government and severe restrictions ordained what newspapers might or might not print. Every cinema had to show at least one Argentine newsreel. In order to pursue its nationalistic policies of building a powerful modern country, the regime had turned Argentina into a conventional military dictatorship. Only the genius of Perón enabled it to gain a broad popular base.

Although Perón was not visible on the Fourth of June, powerful backers and his own intense ambition ensured a rapid rise. General Farrell, who preferred whisky and nightclubs to the dull routine of office, became Minister of War, then vice-president. Perón, his chief aide, was left free to administer the army, where he appointed increasing numbers of the GOU. At the same time, he started to cultivate labour. He let his old friend Mercante, the son of a railway engineer and now military director of the railway union, know that he would be welcome in the war ministry. Through Mercante he met labour leaders and the union lawyer, Juan Bramuglia. On 27 September, Perón asked to be put in charge of the National Labour Department, an obscure office of little consequence; a month later, he got the title of Secretary of Labour and Social Welfare. This became the base for his success, and for the transformation of Argentine society and politics.

Perón followed an activist policy: workers got paid holidays, social security and restrictions on employers' ability to dismiss them. Anti-labour legislation was repealed and the workers, who had been almost universally ignored, were cultivated – a rational policy for a regime that wanted to build up industry. Perón's work paid off in popularity: at a meeting of railway workers in December he was hailed as the nation's First Worker, and on May Day 1944, the General Confederation of Labour (CGT) invited him to speak at their celebrations. Never had labour so honoured an army officer.

At the time of the Revolution, Perón was unknown to the public. Six months later, his voice was becoming familiar, as he took to the radio to announce the government's programme of social welfare. In January 1944, under American pressure, President Ramirez declared war on the Axis. Perón responded by dissolving the GOU, thus releasing its members from their oath of loyalty to Ramirez, who was deposed on 23 February. Farrell became President, with Perón as his War Minister. By July, he had outmanoeuvered his rivals and become Vice-

President. He pleased the army by expanding the officer corps, and giving them increased pay, more promotions and the latest equipment. Secure in the military, the real base of his power, and in the administration, where he held key offices, he could devote his efforts to the social welfare he consistently advocated.

Perón's policy was reminiscent of Mussolini's corporate state, with all public bodies organized and directed by the government. To the employers, he offered security from Communism, and to the workers improved social security and labour courts where they could voice their complaints. But the benefits came at the price of subordination. Perón encouraged the creation of new unions – the government recognized only one per industry – which would be tied to him by the favours they received. Where the workers were recalcitrant, he encouraged rival unions. He gained the powerful meat packers, for example, by supporting the breakaway group of Cipriano Reyes in order to destroy the existing communist union. When Reyes' men went on strike, he made sure they got what they wanted, and marched down the street arm-in-arm with their chief. Concrete actions and incessant self-advertisement made Perón so popular among labour that, when he finally manoeuvered the unions into an expanded CGT, he was recognized as their champion.

Open association with Perón brought Eva Duarte increased fame and influence, and led her to change her image. As a public figure, she needed suitable clothes. She called in a designer who created the sober tweed suit that became her trademark, as well as spectacular gowns for grand occasions. She wore one of them to the opera house on 25 May 1944, at a gala where no minister would ever have brought his mistress, let alone have displayed her openly. Perón, never hesitant to defy conventional opinion, had the perfect mate in Eva whose coarseness could add to the shock of her presence. By now, she had became a blonde; she dyed her hair for a role in a new film, *Circus Cavalcade*, where she made a disagreeable impression. She appeared on the set when she pleased and quarrelled with other actresses, but no one dared confront a colleague who arrived in a government limousine, and whose role, everyone knew, was the result of Perón's control of the film supply. Likewise, no radio star could afford to cross Eva Duarte after she was elected president of the only broadcast union recognized by the government. Her boss was among the first to recognize her new position by giving her a year's contract at an unprecedented salary.

By mid-1944, Eva's voice was heard on all three major stations, especially in a government-backed programme, *Toward A Better Future*, which glorified the Revolution and magnified Perón's role. So far, she had been uninvolved in politics; these programmes were her first lessons. For the rest of her career, she never deviated from the kind of extravagant praise she learned in these scripts. More practical political experience, though, came from living with Perón. Instead of retiring like most wives when important visitors appeared, Eva would receive ministers, officers and union officials, address them in familiar terms and join in the discussions. The more dignified, especially among the officers, came to hate her; for one of them, 'the impudence of that woman reached intolerable heights'. Her colleagues at the radio were no more enthusiastic: one station lost government advertising when a mysterious voice announced 'that tart is on' just before one of Eva's programmes.[1]

In 1945, Perón and his colleagues had much to worry about. The collapse of Nazi Germany provoked three days of popular demonstrations against the regime. Concessions to the universities and the promise of free elections only seemed signs of weakness. The opposition – political parties, Oligarchy and students – was ready to move but lacked a leader. The United States unexpectedly supplied one in Spruille Braden, who arrived as ambassador in April. A successful mining engineer who had grown up in Chile, Braden hated Fascism and rapidly developed a distaste for Perón with whom he had several fruitless and often angry meetings. Braden spoke openly for democracy and against the government in speeches all over the country. The opposition, secure in its support in Buenos Aires, drew inspiration from him, but made the drastic mistake of failing to guarantee the gains recently made by the workers. Perón responded by inflammatory speeches in the workers' suburbs and by trying to accommodate the Radicals, but only a few like Hortensio Quijano and Juan Cooke joined him. His reputation was not helped when two German submarines docked in July and August. Although they were investigated with the co-operation of US intelligence, they stirred fabulous rumours: that Martin Bormann (if not Hitler himself) was aboard, bringing a tremendous treasure to establish a Fourth Reich in Argentina; and that a large part of it went directly to Perón and Eva Duarte, who was suspected of being a German agent. Actually, she was far more concerned with her acting career, where Perón's influence got her the lead role in *La Prodiga*. She incongruously played an older woman famous for her generosity to the poor. Her growing fame, though, did her lover no good, since the opposition's hatred tended to crystallize around her. Perón's situation was becoming critical.

When in August 1945 Farrell lifted the state of siege that had suppressed liberty since 1941, he opened the floodgates to demonstrations and plots. Opposition leaders started planning a coup with the navy (which had always opposed Perón) and with former President Rawson. But first they gave a public demonstration of their power. The peaceful March for the Constitution and Liberty on 19 September drew the biggest crowd in history. It was a great success, though some remarked on the absence of workers. The next week, Rawson's incompetent attempt at a coup gave Farrell the excuse to reimpose the state of siege. That did not stop the students, now in open revolt: 30,000 of them barricaded themselves in the university and held off the police for ten days, a period that would long be remembered as a heady and exciting time when the young took on the regime.

On 1 October, Perón had Eva's friend Nicolini appointed head of the department of Posts and Telegraph, which controlled all forms of communication. This action provoked the greatest crisis of his career. The appointment of a corrupt associate to a post promised to an officer was the last straw for the military, who already despised Eva Duarte's influence. On 6 October, General Avalos, commander of the Campo de Mayo garrison outside the capital, demanded that Perón revoke the appointment. With Eva encouraging him, he refused. After another fruitless meeting, the troops determined to march. On 9 October, Perón received the ultimatum: resign or face a revolt. After ascertaining that Farrell would not back him, Perón resigned from all his posts. This sudden news delighted the opposition as much as it horrified the unions. Perón went home, his career seemingly at an end.

The next day, Reyes, Mercante and Gay (head of the telephone workers) arrived at Perón's apartment and urged him not to give up. Realizing that he had powerful support, he asked Farrell's permission to bid farewell to the workers in the labour ministry. His nationally broadcast speech to a huge crowd announced a general rise for the workers and implicitly asked for their support. The military was so furious that Perón and Eva blockaded themselves in the apartment for a tense night, and left Buenos Aires the following morning. They took refuge on an island, but the police soon found them. Perón, who had to tear himself from an hysterically sobbing Eva, was consigned to Martín García, a remote prison island. From there, he wrote an affectionate letter to Eva, promising her marriage and a quiet life in retirement. After a few days, though, he contrived his return to the military hospital in the capital by claiming ill health.

Meanwhile, Perón's supporters were busy: Reyes, Gay and Mercante's secretary Isabel Ernst roused the unions. Wildcat strikes spread around the capital, while workers angrily demonstrated for Perón throughout the country. On 17 October there was the unprecedented culmination of all this activity. To the shock of its inhabitants, peaceful hordes of workers left their grimy suburbs and poured into the centre of the city where normally they were rarely seen. By nightfall, 300,000 people were clamouring for Perón. Avalos realized that there was no alternative: sending in the troops was out of the question. Only Perón could calm the situation, but his terms were hard: the cabinet must resign and be replaced by his choices. Avalos agreed, and Perón greeted the rapturous throng by torchlight. He gave a temperate impromptu speech, engaged in a dialogue with the crowd and told them all to take the next day off as a holiday.

The crowd dispersed peacefully, and Perón finally went home to Eva. On 22 October, he married her in a civil ceremony, with a church service on 10 December. Their wedding certificate was full of lies, most notably that Eva was born in 1922, apparently in an effort to make her look legitimate. More effectively, her original birth certificate, which gave the name Ibarguren not Duarte, was removed from the local register and a fake inserted. From this time on, Eva's early life was a forbidden subject and her acting career was at an end.

The Seventeenth of October became the great holiday of the Peronists who built many myths around it, including a heroic role for Eva who actually did nothing. Within a few days Perón's working-class supporters were called *descamisados*, 'shirtless ones', an insulting term applied to them because many had taken off their jackets and even their shirts and bathed in the fountains of elegant and formally dressed Buenos Aires. Perón appropriated the term for his followers and proceeded to take off his jacket whenever he addressed them. The day changed Argentina forever; the workers, who had essentially occupied the capital, became a serious force that no government could ignore.

On 13 November, the government announced the elections for 24 February 1946. Perón now immersed himself in democratic politics. Gay and Reyes formed a Labour Party that provided a base, which was joined by a coalition of breakaway Radicals and nationalists. Perón had deep popular support and experienced politicians on his team. The opposition, confident that it would win after years of repression, nominated an uninspiring doctor, José Tamborini, who ran on the slogan 'For Liberty, against Nazism'. Perón picked the respectable and docile Quijano as his running mate, while Mercante filled his old post at the Ministry of Labour, ensuring good relations with the unions. He also received substantial support from outside, including some from an unexpected quarter.

Catholic bishops told their congregations not to vote for anyone who favoured divorce or the ending of religious instruction in the schools – policies advocated only by the liberal opposition. On 20 December, the government granted a general salary increase, a month's bonus for Christmas and paid vacations, a programme that put the opposition in a hopeless quandary. But, best of all, only two weeks before the election, the US State Department published its Blue Book recounting alleged Nazi activities in Argentina. Perón responded at a huge rally the next day, accusing the opposition of being in league with foreigners. His followers immediately took up the extremely effective cry, 'Perón or Braden'. Eva proved an ideal asset in the campaign. As she rode in Perón's train, she reached out to touch the people, an activity that Perón avoided. It was the first time a candidate's wife had played such a role; the crowds loved it. Although the campaign was relatively peaceful, Tamborini's battered train limped back to the capital with several bullet holes. The election itself was the cleanest in decades. Perón won 52 per cent of the vote, but got two-thirds of the Deputies, and all but two Senators. He had the mandate to remake the country as he wished.

In the month before the inauguration, Farrell's government passed bills that showed the direction of the new Perón administration. It broadened social security, with old-age pensions and worker's compensation; lifted the state of siege; and laid the foundations for a planned economy by nationalizing the central bank and creating the Argentine Institute for Trade Promotion (IAPI), which would play a dominant role in the economy. True to its old form, it also intervened in the universities.

On 4 June 1946, the third anniversary of the Revolution, Perón was inaugurated as President of Argentina. He wore his general's uniform, reflecting the promotion that took effect a week earlier. At the inaugural banquet, Eva wore a dress with a bare shoulder that, to widespread scandal, was turned toward the unsmiling Cardinal Coppello. The presidential couple then retired to their 283-room official residence, where Perón raced a friend down the banister while Eva sat on the bed in her pyjamas eating an orange.

FOUR

THE JOINT DICTATORSHIP, 1946–9

A free, just and independent Argentina was Perón's announced goal. Abundant popular support, firm control of the army and government and an immensely rich country gave him the means to achieve it. Freedom, though, had a special meaning for Perón. His popularity would have allowed him to operate a democracy, but his training and temperament inclined him to dictatorship. Perón moved systematically against all rival centres of power until he had reduced the population to complete subjection. For nine years, he was successful, until he took on a rival he could not defeat.

Perón's twin bases were the army and labour. The army posed no problem: its numbers doubled, its officers got higher pay than their American counterparts and it had the most modern equipment. Labour had a mind of its own, but its leaders were no match for Perón. Shortly before his inauguration, he merged his coalition, including the Labour Party, into a Sole Party of the Revolution. His old backers, Reyes and Gay, resigned. Gay was elected head of the CGT in November, but his victory was short-lived. In January 1947, a delegation of the American AFL arrived to investigate labour conditions. They met with Gay in a room that Perón's police had bugged. The resultant accusation of plotting with the Americans to suborn the CGT forced Gay to resign. Within a year, the CGT fell to the obsequious José Espejo, reportedly the former doorman of Eva's apartment building. The outspoken Reyes, who remained in opposition, had a harder fate. He was arrested in September 1948, accused of participating in an American plot against the government and never released while Perón was in office. With the eclipse of these two early supporters, Perón's hold over labour was secure.

Perón controlled the government through his Sole Party. He made all final decisions and could veto any candidate. Members were carefully screened and indoctrinated; their numbers were secret, but probably reached 250,000 to 300,000. Party leaders took special courses, some taught by Perón and Eva themselves. In 1949, the Sole Party appropriately became the Peronist Party. In Congress, it formed a monolithic block that commanded every vote. It could afford to let the opposition speak and object, especially since they were divided. Yet even this illusion of democracy had limits, for outspoken opposition could lead to loss of immunity or expulsion. Even more chilling was the law on disrespect passed in October. Its terms were so vague that any suspicious or irreverent comment might result in imprisonment.

The courts and the press are natural defenders of freedom; Perón swiftly dealt with them. In October 1946, he had the Supreme Court impeached, not because they opposed his measures, but on the supremely ironic grounds that they had recognized the revolutionary government. The justices were removed from office on May Day 1947, and replaced by docile successors, who included Eva's brother-in-law. The press did not give in as easily. Perón attacked it on several fronts. Harassed by obscure regulations and government inspectors, many unfriendly papers gave up publication or abandoned opposition. Only

La Prensa, the unyielding voice of the opposition, continued publishing despite a desperate shortage of the newsprint that the government controlled. Eva also played a role. With a loan from the recently nationalized Central Bank and the help of her friend the shipping magnate Alberto Dodero, she bought the paper *Democracia* early in 1947. It became the major organ of government publicity, constantly featuring Eva in articles and photographs. She and her friends then formed a corporation that bought up most of the capital's papers, as well as a radio network and numerous magazines. They all followed the Peronist line.

The universities also succumbed. In 1947, they were put under rectors appointed by the government and forbidden to engage in political activity; 70 per cent of the professors had been purged. Yet in 1949, fees were abolished and higher education opened to all who could qualify. Such actions reflect the ambiguity of Perón's democratic dictatorship. It had no concentration camps and allowed foreign journalists to travel freely, yet they reported an atmosphere of dejection and fear, the products of government control. Late in 1948, a National Register started to keep track of all citizens, who were required to carry official identification and a sinister document, the Good Conduct, essential for employment, study, travel or marriage. If the police took it for any reason, there were serious problems.

Justice for Perón meant social justice, the policies that had already assured his popularity. To achieve it, he had the best team he ever assembled, with labour leaders, technocrats and financial experts. On the other hand, Eva's friend Nicolini returned to his ministry and her unqualified brother, Juan Duarte, became Perón's private secretary. If Eva used nepotism, Perón avoided it: the best job his brother could acquire was director of the Buenos Aires zoo. The crucial position, though, was the Ministry of Labour and Social Welfare. Perón himself could no longer handle it, but he could not afford to appoint anyone who might try to establish his own popular base. Yet at the same time, he wanted to expand social welfare. He found the ideal solution, one which left a permanent mark on Argentina: he appointed the harmless José Freire to the ministry, but allowed Eva to run it. She and Perón gave new meaning to the word 'justice'.

For Perón, independence meant ending foreign dominance of Argentina's economy and building a powerful and modern country. This demanded money and planning. An accumulated surplus of $1.6 billion provided a good start, but a permanent source of capital was necessary. For that, he used the newly formed IAPI, which bought the country's agricultural products at low prices and sold them abroad at a high profit. To organize his programme, he adopted a Five-Year Plan in September 1946; it called for a much greater state role in the economy and introduced a cult of work, to be led by Argentina's First Worker.

On 9 September 1947, in Tucumán, where Argentina's political independence had been declared, Perón rather prematurely proclaimed the country's economic independence. He had already nationalized several public utilities, but the best was yet to come. On 1 March 1948, Perón announced his acquisition of the British-owned railway system to a crowd of an estimated one million people. Finally, transport was in Argentine hands, and the leader could adopt his favorite slogan, *Perón Cumple*, 'Perón gets it done', to which *Eva dignifica*, 'Eva dignifies' was soon added. With or without dignity, the railways were a bad deal: the British extracted an enormous price for the decrepit lines which soaked up huge subsidies and served as a major source of employment for the party faithful.

The dictator himself, called 'Leader' or 'Conductor', maintained his unfailing courtesy and military discipline. He regularly arrived at his office at 6.20 a.m., signed papers until 7, received visitors till noon then he went home for lunch with Eva. After a siesta, he returned to work at 4 p.m. and stayed until 8 or 9 before returning to the Residence for dinner. He later claimed that in nine years as president he was only late once. Perón's tastes were simple: he had no interest in luxury or rich food, loved his poodles and enjoyed spending relaxing, simple weekends in the country with Eva, who made the beds while Perón cooked the meals. He liked boxing matches, western movies, tango music and fast cars. He never lost his love of sports and the young. This simple Perón, so like the common people, was a natural mass leader. But he had a more devious and complex side. However charming he might be, Perón never became anyone's friend and was always willing to sacrifice his close associates. His unfailing smile hid a deeply manipulative nature which he expressed well: 'I manage things best in a *quilombo*' (literally, a whorehouse, meaning a state of confusion).[1] He always sowed division to keep opposition or followers off balance. There was a third side, the intellectual: Perón wrote a weekly column in *Democracia* and gave lectures at the Peronist school which were later collected into a book, *Political Leadership* (1951). Organization, intelligence, hard work and deceit had always been his characteristics.

Perón and Eva complemented each other perfectly. He was the statesman, above routine details of administration; she was direct, outspoken and passionate, throwing herself into every aspect of her work. He disliked physical contact; she embraced everyone. His ideology was fluid; she was a fanatic believer. He presided calmly but ruthlessly over the dictatorship; she practiced and preached a doctrine of love for the humble. As her power grew, her schedule diverged from Perón's. She would rise later than he, hold audiences at the Residence until mid-morning, then work in her office until late at night, with a break for lunch at home. Later, she tended to take lunch in town and sometimes did not return until Perón was getting up from his siesta. They formed an unbeatable team.

Eva's was the kind face of the regime, dealing with social welfare and matters that concerned women. She campaigned energetically for female suffrage and took full credit when it was granted in September 1947. But she was no feminist: she always maintained that women should follow traditional roles centred on husbands and families, though they could participate in politics, as she did. Already before Perón's inauguration, she started visiting factories and gave her first speech to a labour group. Soon after it, she took an office in Nicolini's ministry, and met union delegates. Contact with the unions increased when she moved into Perón's old office at the Ministry of Labour in September 1946, not in any official position, but merely as her husband's representative. Since Perón was usually busy, union leaders came to her. At first, she was ignorant and hesitant, depending heavily on her advisers. Gradually, as she gained confidence, she developed a real rapport with the workers and their leaders. She soon became the dispenser of welfare and social justice to her beloved *descamisados*.

Charity had been the province of society ladies who normally asked the president's wife to officiate. When the prospect of Eva was too much for them, they told her politely that she was too young. She replied by suggesting that they name her mother. Actually, the ladies' charitable society was already moribund and heavily subsidized by the government when Perón abolished it in September 1946. He concentrated all social welfare in the Labour Ministry, where Eva took charge. Her job brought her close to the poor, whose plight she understood all too well from her own experience. At first, she would drive to factories and packing plants in a truck, distributing food and clothing. Then letters requesting help began to pour in along with donations from unions and individuals. Eva had the goods stored at the Residence, where she would sort and package them long after Perón was asleep. This informal beginning led to her greatest role, but first Eva became a star on the broader stage of Europe.

Early in 1947, Francisco Franco, the Spanish dictator who had few friends beside Argentina, invited Perón for a state visit; he declined, but proposed to send Eva. That suited her, for she had long dreamed of Europe and of the annual sojourns there of the Argentine Oligarchy. Armed with an enormous wardrobe and suitable retinue she landed in Madrid on 8 June 1947. The Caudillo himself met her at the airport, and the streets were lined with millions of Spaniards excited by the glamour and wealth that passed before them. For a battered

Europe, she represented hope from the New World. During her triumphal two-week stay, she toured Spain, received magnificent gifts, attended innumerable receptions and lectured Franco, and anyone else who would listen, about Argentina's progress in social welfare. Small talk was not her strong point in such unfamiliar and intimidating surroundings. At first, she was so frightened that she made her companion and adviser, Lilian Guardo, sleep in her room. Gradually, though, as she was received with universal enthusiasm, she developed more poise and announced that she had come as a rainbow between the two countries, a phrase that produced the name 'Rainbow Tour'. After Spain, Italy was a disappointment: her audience with the Pope yielded a rosary instead of a papal title, and dissident communists heckled her speech. When she learned that no invitation to Buckingham Palace was forthcoming, she cancelled a planned visit to England. In Paris, though, she charmed everyone she met, then made a mysterious excursion to Switzerland. Enemies claimed she went there to deposit stolen money in anonymous accounts, but more plausibly she wanted to make contact with German scientists who could be useful to

The official portrait of Eva against the background of a titanic crowd demanding her as Vice-President, 1951. (Published in the Party magazine, *Mundo Peronista*/Hoover Institution Library)

All eyes are on Evita as she and Juan receive the delegates of the Printers' Union, 1947. (Hoover Institution Archives)

Mutual understanding: Juan and Eva in the presidential palace, 1948. (Hoover Institution Archives)

Fiery words: Eva in her characteristic tweed suit addressing the crowd, *c.* 1950. (Published in the Party magazine, *Mundo Peronista* / Hoover Institution Library)

Favourite activity: a businessman hands Eva 50,000 pesos for the Foundation, 1951.
(Hoover Institution Archives)

Centres of power: the
neoclassical Eva Perón
Foundation building in front of
the headquarters of the trade
union federation, the CGT.
(The author)

Mi hermanita y yo, amamos a
mamá, papá, Perón y Evita.

'My little sister and I love mama, papa, Perón and Evita': a happy Peronist family from an elementary school reader of 1953. (Hoover Institution Library)

1° DE MAYO
FIESTA DE LOS

The Workers' Heroes: images of Evita and Perón dominate the May Day celebrations of 1953. (Published in the Party magazine, *Mundo Peronista*/Hoover Institution Library)

Eva Duarte: a publicity photograph of Eva the actress reproduced in the Peronist calendar for 1953. (Hoover Institution Archives)

The Dictator: Perón looms over the national sports meeting in 1955. (Published in the Party magazine, *Mundo Peronista*/Hoover Institution Library)

Spreading the word: local headquarters of Eva's Peronist Women's Party. (Published in the Party magazine, *Mundo Peronista*/Hoover Institution Library)

Fatal temptation: Perón and the girls' basketball team of the UES, 1955. (Published in the Party magazine, *Mundo Peronista*/Hoover Institution Library)

Working in exile: Perón communicating with the faithful from Spain, with Eva's image close at hand, 1960. (Hoover Institution Archives)

Taller than Liberty or Christ: the proposed monument for Eva Perón. (*Monumento a Eva Perón*)

Perón as Moses: proposed statue for Eva's monument, celebrating Perón's granting the Workers' Ten Rights in 1947, the cornerstone of his programme. (*Monumento a Eva Perón*)

also had her own faction: her brother controlled access to Perón, one brother-in-law sat on the Supreme Court, another was director of Customs; the pliable ministers Freire and Nicolini were loyal allies, as were Espejo, who ran the CGT, and Raúl Apold, director of broadcasting and a source of constant praise. For finances she could always count on Dodero, and for ultimate backing on Perón. However powerful she seemed, she had no base but him, and did nothing of which he disapproved.

Perón's Argentina was making its presence felt in other parts of the world. His foreign minister, Juan Bramuglia, gained universal acclaim when he presided judiciously over the UN Security Council during the Berlin blockade in 1948. On a less public level, Perón sought influence abroad by subsidizing journalists and labour groups. His stand for social justice and against US imperialism also appealed to radical students. His men were therefore able to recruit student leaders from Cuba, among them a young Fidel Castro, for a meeting in Bogota, planned for April 1948. Unfortunately for Perón, the city was devastated by a revolution (which Castro happily joined) and his meeting was never held. He had no further contact with Fidel for many years.

FIVE

CONSTITUTION, FOUNDATION, RENUNCIATION, 1949–51

By 1949, Perón was secure: congressional elections the previous March had given him two-thirds of the Deputies and all the Senators, the army and unions were content, Eva's activities were generating widespread popularity, and the opposition rarely risked raising its head. Perón could now plan for a permanent legacy, a new constitution that would recognize all the progress made since the Revolution. The document that Congress approved in March enshrined a greater role for the state, but promised civil liberties, with the ambiguous exception that 'the state does not recognize the freedom to violate freedom'. It guaranteed specific rights for workers, families and the old; the right to a free education which, however, must inculcate proper Argentine values; the right to private property, though it must recognize social obligations; and the inalienable government ownership of minerals and petroleum. It also allowed the president to be re-elected. Perón was free to run the country as long as he pleased.

Perón's reforms were soon overshadowed by the activities of his wife. Evita (she liked to use this familiar form) threw her phenomenal energy into the struggle for social justice. Her innumerable speeches, effective and emotional, usually began 'My dear *descamisados*' and overflowed with love for the humble and praise of Perón. She made long working trips around the country. But she especially devoted herself to the Maria Eva Duarte de Perón Social Aid Foundation, founded on 8 July 1948; and more simply called the Eva Perón Foundation from 1949. The shorter name suited her new image. In sober suits or dresses, with her blonde hair pulled back in a severe businesslike style, she was ready to take on the problems of her people.

The Foundation, a private corporation that functioned like a branch of the government, existed to help the poor. It was authorized to build houses, schools, hospitals or anything else the people needed; its projects took priority over all others. By 1950, it was bigger than most ministries: it employed 14,000 people (including 6,000 construction workers and 26 priests) and had assets of some $200,000,000. Every year, it bought 500,000 sewing machines, 400,000 pairs of shoes and 200,000 cooking pots. At Christmas, it distributed 5,000,000 toys and 4,000,000 cakes and bottles of cider. The Foundation was a state within the state, the closest contact between the government and the people, and the generator of phenomenal propaganda and popularity.

Evita, who had absolute control, claimed that she kept no accounts of the vast sums that passed through her hands. Revenues came from the unions, the government, corporations and individuals; the Foundation paid no tax. In 1953, it received $30,000,000 in cash, a corresponding sum from the government and $6,000,000 from labour. The Foundation got 20 per cent of the profits of the state lottery and a share of the taxes on cinema tickets, horse races and, its critics maintained, whorehouses. Periodically, Congress would vote special appropriations. The biggest windfall, 97 million pesos, came when the Supreme Court ruled against the phenomenally rich Bemberg family in a long-standing tax dispute. According to rumour, the Bembergs lost their case because they had supplied Paris newspapers with old photographs of a semi-nude Eva Duarte during the Rainbow Tour.

The papers listed contributions to the Foundation, whether by individuals, companies or trade unions. The unions had a regular procedure. When they wanted something, they would stage a public demonstration, then approach Eva with gifts for the Foundation. She would respond suitably. Supposedly, when the unions asked for an increase of, say 30 to 40 per cent, Eva would get them 50 or 60 per cent, then demand a substantial share for the Foundation. By 1949, a regular procedure was established: the workers would give the first two weeks of their rise and two days' pay a year to the Foundation. This kept everyone happy, but inevitably contributed to the inflation that would undermine Argentina's heady prosperity.

Big businesses were expected to show a generosity that might bring them material benefits, but the reluctant could suffer. In 1950, the anti-

Peronist head of Argentina's leading pharmaceutical firm refused to supply free vaccines to the Foundation. His electricity was shut off, then inspectors closed the factory because it contained spoiled products. He fled to exile in Uruguay. Similarly, the Mu-Mu company that made sweets that all children loved, rashly presented the Foundation with a bill instead of a donation. Inspectors swiftly discovered rat hairs in the vats and closed the factory. These cases received widespread notoriety, but they seem to have been the only ones of their kind.

Personal attention to the poor was Eva's best publicity. Every day, her office was jammed with peasant women, squalling children, old folks, union members and government officials anxious to explain their problems, while others waited in a long queue outside. Eva would listen patiently, offer a solution that might be anything from a sewing machine to a new house, and hand the petitioner a 50-peso bill for the fare home. She often gave more than was asked, since she knew the poor could be shy and hesitant in their requests. She was unfailingly attentive and sympathetic, embracing all of them, even if they were leprous or covered with sores. Officials and ministers, though, had to wait their turn and were often called on to empty their wallets for the poor. Eva never left her office till the last supplicant had been heard, even if it meant staying half the night.

Each day, Eva saw hundreds of people. Radio and the press encouraged the public to write to the Foundation; they responded with 12,000 letters a day. The lucky ones received an appointment. Likewise, when Eva appeared at the theatre, she would be showered with slips of paper bearing the names of people who wanted to see her. These, too, could lead to interviews. The cases chosen formed a representative selection of problems. Good Peronists were likely to receive the largest rewards, but others were not excluded, for a gift to a non-supporter could often make a convert. Although the whole process was derided as a lottery, it had a real effect. Never had a government shown such direct attention to the poor, and never had such a glamorous woman devoted her days and nights to their welfare. Every sewing machine or bed that was distributed was a source of propaganda, for news of the generosity would rapidly spread. More than forty years after Evita's death, people were still talking with feeling of the gifts they or someone they knew had received.

Direct help was only part of the Foundation's work. It also built hospitals — usually in working-class districts — schools, homes for the elderly, resort hotels for the workers, an entire village for children, transit homes for women and children, and a home for girls who, like Eva herself, had left their families to look for work in the city. Evita often arrived unannounced to inspect her establishments. Most were built in a luxurious style to show the poor that they were entitled to the best, just as Eva wore lavish clothes and jewellery. She always maintained that everything she had belonged to the poor and never denied that she had once been one of them (though she never gave any details). She also founded a school for nurses, offering free tuition and four years' training to 1,300 women ready to practice in remote areas where doctors were rare. The Foundation made its resources available to everyone, with little or no charge, and even rushed emergency aid to foreign countries, usually in Latin America, but on one embarrassing occasion, to Washington, DC.

Eva put Perón's love of sports and the young into practice in the Children's Football Championship.

Every community was encouraged to form a team, for which the Foundation would supply uniforms and equipment. This was another form of social welfare: it provided activities for real or potential delinquents and looked after their health. When the teams were organized, the Foundation would give them physical examinations and X-rays, often for the first time in their lives. At the championship play-offs in Buenos Aires, Eva would kick the first ball, and award the prizes which usually included land and a new clubhouse. By these means, physical education spread throughout the country.

Eva's activities naturally included politics. In July 1949, she founded the Women's Peronist Party, to create a body of politically aware and active women who, like her, would understand that 'for a woman, to be a Peronist, means above all, loyalty to Perón, subordination to Perón, and blind trust in Perón'.[1] This was more like missionary work than feminism. The Party was an enormous success: by 1952, it had 500,000 members and 3,600 headquarters where neighbourhood women could learn useful skills. Eva herself taught proper diction to the Party leaders. These women were a major factor in Perón's re-election, and the Women's organization that reached everywhere enabled him to keep better control of the country, house by house.

Generosity made Eva no less vindictive towards her enemies, such as Ernesto Sammartino who denounced dictatorship in the Congress in August 1948: 'We have not come here to bow reverently before the whip or to dance jigs to please a Madame Pompadour. This is not a fashionable night club or the anteroom of a palace'.[2] The indiscreet reference earned Sammartino immediate expulsion; he prudently fled to Uruguay. Late in 1949, the Spanish ambassador resigned when Eva insulted him; but her action was calculated because she heard that he had spoken ill of her at dinner. Eva had spies everywhere, especially among domestic servants, waiters and taxi drivers, who would all rush to tell the Señora anything derogatory.

No one was safe, not even the widely respected Bramuglia. Eva had hated him since October 1945 when he had refused to file for habeas corpus for Perón on the grounds that he would ruin his cause if he left the country. He had also opposed the Rainbow Tour because it might complicate relations with the United States. Eva's newspapers never mentioned him and even erased his image from photographs. He finally resigned in August 1949. Perón's best friend Mercante also lost her favour, either because he was reluctant to change the constitution to allow Perón's re-election, or because he wanted to be vice-president, a post she coveted. He stayed on as governor of Buenos Aires, but never regained influence.

Eva seemed to have unlimited power, but she really acted in Perón's interests. Her role allowed him to remain above the strife, to shake his head in sadness, while she did what he wanted. Bramuglia and Mercante, for example, were very popular among the railway workers and potential leaders of the Party. Since Perón had no loyalty to friends nor any desire to encourage rivals, allowing Eva to remove them solved potential problems while leaving him free from blame.

Sacking popular leaders, however, involved risks, especially at a time of economic problems. By 1950, factors beyond Perón's control – Europe was producing more of its own food, and a terrible drought hit Argentina – brought economic problems, while uncontrolled government spending was driving an inflation that eroded the workers' gains. Trouble began late in 1950 with a series of railway strikes. Neither the CGT nor Eva's personal pleadings could calm the workers who even scrawled an unthinkable slogan on the walls: 'Long Live Perón the Widower'! Perón solved the problem by drafting the workers into the army and subjecting them to military discipline. The regime was becoming even more authoritarian. A strengthened law of disrespect abolished the truth as a defence; and new laws on treason, sabotage and espionage were so vague that they could be used against any form of dissent. Yet Perón typically passed the Statute of the Peon which gave rural workers greater rights than ever, while the Foundation was constantly creating goodwill for the regime.

The remaining voice of freedom, the newspaper *La Prensa*, had accurately reported the railway strike, much to the Peróns' indignation. Eva especially hated it because it never referred to her by name or covered her social occasions; she vowed to 'make them pay for all the suffering they caused the poor'.[3] A Peronist mob had already attacked the paper in 1947, but now it was time to end freedom of the press. In January 1951, the paper was closed, then expropriated and turned

transport, food and lodging and a general strike enabled all to attend. On 22 August 1951, a crowd estimated at a million filled the vast July 7th Avenue beneath 60-ft tall portraits of Perón and Eva. Cries of 'Evita' brought their heroine to the stage where she gave a speech full of venom for the Oligarchy and love for her *descamisados* but said nothing about running for office. The crowd demanded an answer, engaging her in a long dialogue that ended in her vague promise to do what the people wanted. The meeting was not following its script. The people were determined to have Evita as their candidate, but she somehow was unable to accept. On 31 August, in a moving radio broadcast, Eva finally announced her irrevocable decision not to be a candidate. She recalled the Seventeenth of October and the best years of her life, spent with her 'master and friend, General Perón', but said she had only one ambition: that history would say 'there was a woman at Perón's side who dedicated herself to bringing to him the hopes of the people that Perón then converted into beautiful reality; and that the people lovingly called that woman, Evita'. She renounced honours, not the struggle: 'I will follow him as his most humble collaborator, occupying the post of battle where I serve the people as one of them and General Perón as a Peronist'.[4] She thanked her supporters but repeated her refusal.

There are many explanations for Eva's renunciation. For some, Perón did not want her as Vice-President since her present role suited him best; others believe that he knew she was fatally ill. Most probably, Perón yielded to an ultimatum from the army, which never accepted Eva and certainly did not want her as their commander-in-chief if he ceased to be President. Whatever had happened, Evita's star was beginning to set.

EVITA'S DEATH, PERÓN'S FALL, 1951–5

Within a month of her renunciation, Eva was confined to bed. Perón was told that she had cancer; she never was. The public, who learned only that she was seriously ill, showed their sympathy with ever deeper degrees of passion. Eva's slow demise became the central event in Argentina.

On 28 September 1951, an ineffectual coup gave Perón the excuse for further repression: public meetings were restricted, and radio could be used only for transmitting information, not political messages (Peronist broadcasts were considered informational). This coincided with the presidential campaign where one of the opposition candidates was arrested and another shot. Eva also reacted to the political unrest. The day after the coup, she summoned Espejo to her bedside and ordered him secretly to buy 5,000 automatic pistols and 1,500 machine guns for a proposed workers' militia. On 15 October, her 'autobiography', *La Razón de mi Vida (The Account of My Life)*, was published. It sold 150,000 copies the first day and within a month had broken all records for an Argentine book. This vapid ghost-written production, a work of propaganda that revealed virtually nothing about Evita, became required reading in the schools.

Under heavy sedation, Eva attended the Seventeenth of October celebrations where she received the Grand Peronist medal loaded with emeralds. On 6 November, she underwent a hysterectomy in her Foundation's Presidente Perón hospital while a crowd of 20,000 kept vigil outside. Since she was still too weak to move on election day, 11 November, a special law allowed her to cast her ballot in her hospital bed. Eva had proclaimed that anyone who did not vote for Perón was a traitor. There were few of them: Perón got 64 per cent of the vote; all the governors and Senators and 90 per cent of the Deputies elected were Peronists.

By Christmas, Eva was able to hand out presents at the Residence, and may have been cheered in the new year when the territory of Chaco became known as Eva Perón province, but in February her abdominal pains returned and she began to lose weight rapidly. Yet she never lost the determination that still gave her power. In March, the unpopular Espejo was narrowly defeated for re-election as head of the CGT. Her supporters locked the delegates in the room and rushed to telephone the Señora. When she told them what she thought, they re-elected Espejo unanimously.

She addressed her *descamisados* for the last time on May Day. After crediting Perón for raising the banner of redemption and justice, she turned to 'treacherous vipers': 'I ask God not to let those idiots raise a hand against Perón because – woe be that day! – on that day I shall go forth with the working people, I shall go forth with the women of the people, I shall go forth with the *descamisados* of the Fatherland, so as not to leave standing a single brick that is not Peronist.' But love accompanied rage: 'I am with you in the fight again . . . like yesterday, today and tomorrow; I am with you to be a rainbow of love between the people and Perón.'[1]

Perón had to carry her from the balcony. The next week, on her thirty-third birthday, she received the title 'Spiritual Chief of the Nation'.

Eva refused to miss Perón's inauguration on 4 June. Shot full of painkiller, weighing only 80 pounds and supported by a special frame that her fur coat concealed, she waved to the admiring crowds. They never saw her again. With her obvious deterioration, the public was becoming frantic. Her followers attended constant masses and vigils, while respectable ladies kept their daughters away from the doctor because of the rumour that Eva needed constant transfusions of fresh young blood.

In June, Congress authorized the construction of a vast monument to Eva; it was to contain her body, which Perón ordered embalmed by a Spanish specialist, Dr Pedro Ara. On 18 July, when she was at the edge of consciousness, Eva received the diamond-laden Collar of San Martin, which gave her the right to a state funeral. By now, the Residence was surrounded by weeping women on their knees and vast crowds attended an open-air mass for her recovery. But all was in vain: on 26 July 1952, at 8.25 p.m., Eva Perón officially entered immortality. She was thirty-three years old; she had been a public figure for a decade.

While Argentina stood still, Dr Ara rushed to prepare the body for public display. Enormous grief-stricken crowds waited to bid farewell in queues that stretched for thirty blocks, while Perón stood silently by the coffin. On 10 August, the President, Eva's family and the government followed the thirty-nine union members who drew the coffin on a gun carriage in slow procession past files of soldiers and 2 million spectators. Many of them might have supported the unions who asked the Pope to begin proceedings for Eva's canonization.

Eva's faction followed her into oblivion. Within a few months, Espejo, Cámpora and Freire the Labour Minister were forced out. When Perón expelled Mercante, who had hopes for a comeback, from the Party, he showed that he was uprooting potential leaders as well as Eva's friends. The heaviest blow fell on Eva's brother Juan, a notorious playboy who boasted of having a fortune of a billion pesos. The new CGT head and others complained about him just as Perón was attacking corruption. Duarte, put under investigation, resigned from the cabinet. He was found dead in his apartment on

9 April 1953. Although Duarte left a suicide note, many believed he had been murdered. Cynics associated it with his recent trip to Europe; they believed he had been sent to retrieve Eva's legendary holdings in Switzerland, but had either failed to find them or squandered the money.

Meanwhile, Perón was making bold moves. In October 1952, he announced his second Five Year plan which combined cuts with increased efforts to bring as many activities as possible under his control. He also tried to increase co-operation with neighbouring countries. A state visit to Chile, however, foundered when it appeared that he really had Argentine domination in mind. Similar efforts directed at other neighbours produced few concrete results, but reflected his old policy of creating a strong South American block to resist US influence. This all changed after Perón received a visit from Milton Eisenhower, brother of the newly elected president, in April 1953. Suddenly, he started to advocate co-operation with the United States and to encourage foreign investment. Argentina badly needed foreign capital to alleviate its economic problems: low agricultural prices, shortage of funds for industrialization and government extravagance had led to a declining standard of living, while emergency measures that froze prices and wages were only a palliative.

So far, Perón seemed to be managing, but events soon took violent and perverse turns that devastated his reputation. The trouble began on 15 April 1953, at a loyalty demonstration organized by the CGT. Bombs interrupted Perón's speech, killing five people. When he resumed talking, he reportedly encouraged the excited crowd to take revenge, but ended on a note of calm. Most went home, but some fanatics laid siege to the Socialist headquarters and burned it; they then proceeded to the Jockey Club, bastion of the Oligarchy, which they looted and destroyed. Perón blamed the Radicals, arrested their leader Balbín and nationalized the Club. He then adopted a conciliatory tone and even proclaimed a general amnesty for Christmas. For the moment, calm seemed to be restored.

On 26 July, the first anniversary of Evita's death, Dr Ara announced that her body was now incorruptible. Final plans for the monument were unveiled: it would be taller than the Statue of Liberty in New York, and crowned by the titanic statue of a *descamisado* who looked remarkably like

Perón. The body was to be kept under guard in CGT headquarters until the monument was ready.

University students had always been an irritation for Perón. In mid-1953, he found a novel solution: a Union of Secondary School Students (UES) would inculcate Peronist ideals into the young before they attended university. Since Argentinians jealously guarded the domain of the family, the organization would focus on sports. Opposition could be expected from the Church, which had its own youth groups, but Perón approved the idea, and even offered the use of his suburban residence for the girls' branch.

By October, the house was filled with hundreds of teenage girls wearing shorts. Perón would greet them when they arrived, order lunch for them and give them lessons in fencing, swimming and riding the motorbike. He often spent the afternoon in this congenial atmosphere, before sending the girls home to their mothers. His behaviour was generally correct, except in the case of Nelly Rivas, the fourteen-year-old daughter of a janitor. She started helping him with chores, then spending the night at the Residence and finally moved in. Nelly stayed with him openly for the next two years. Perón had always enjoyed the company of younger women and loved to flaunt social conventions, but for most people this was simply too much.

These activities led to horrendous rumours. Perón's enemies reported that the Residence was the scene of orgies; that the Leader lured the girls there by offering them motorbike lessons, then used Eva's jewellery in order to seduce them. A whole genre of spurious 'memoirs' appeared, making Perón the subject of pornography. Although the laws of disrespect muted public criticism, no one could miss the President's bizarre behaviour as he sped down the streets of the capital on a motorbike with a flock of teenage girls behind him. His reputation never recovered.

Outward harmony continued into 1954. The congressional elections in April gave the Peronists a record 69 per cent of the vote and the economic situation seemed to be easing. Foreign investment increased, Perón bought a steel mill from the United States and entered into negotiations with the American magnate Henry J. Kaiser for an automobile factory. He was advised by a rich businessman, Jorge Antonio, who unsuccessfully demanded a large fee for his rather dubious role in that transaction.

In July, a group of Catholics founded a Christian Democratic party, a small group that Perón considered to be a real threat. Then, when Catholic Action began to compete successfully with the UES, Perón started to attack the Church. No one knows why he embarked on the campaign that would destroy him. He had always been on good terms with the Church, which had given him valuable support. Yet the Church was the one corporate body that stood outside his control. Perhaps Perón feared that Catholic influence might impede his party's activities; perhaps he was too distracted to think realistically; perhaps, as he later maintained, he was badly advised. In any case, he moved to the attack on Loyalty Day (17 October), denouncing politicians, communists and wolves in sheeps' clothing, which everyone took as a reference to the clergy. A month later, it was the turn of Catholic Action, as well as unnamed priests, bishops and the clergy. At one of his speeches, the crowd bore banners proclaiming 'Perón yes! Priests no!' and Delia Parodi of the Women's Party announced 'many roads lead to Rome but *every* road leads to Perón'.[2]

The attack grew fiercer in December: Congress legalized divorce and prostitution, and gave full rights to illegitimate children. Argentine Catholics, not famed for their devotion to the Church, responded in force, but peacefully: the 200,000 who attended the feast of the Immaculate Conception in December were clearly making a political statement. It led to a ban on religious demonstrations that drove resistance underground. Catholic leaders began to contact dissident army and navy officers, while a clandestine wave of pamphlets attacked Perón, corruption and the UES. Evita alone was spared.

In April 1955, the government announced an agreement with Standard Oil of California to exploit a vast tract of Patagonia under highly favourable terms. This reversal of policy (in violation of Perón's own constitution) was so stunning that even the subservient Peronists in Congress hesitated to vote for it. The concessions, however justified economically, roused widespread nationalist feelings against Perón. Antagonism grew in May when Congress abolished religious instruction in the schools, proposed to tax Church property and called for a convention to separate Church and state.

June brought disaster. On the 11th, a huge demonstration to celebrate Corpus Christi day plainly had politics in mind, as people carried the yellow flag of the Vatican. Although they dispersed peacefully, the government claimed in screaming headlines that some of them had burned the Argentine flag. Congress met in special session, the CGT rallied and Perón deported two Argentine priests to Italy. Rome responded with its most powerful weapon: excommunication for those responsible for the expulsion, though none were specifically named.

The day of the excommunication, 16 June, turned into a day of infamy. The navy revolted, sending planes in to bomb the Casa Rosada. They scored direct hits, but failed to kill Perón. Instead, over 350 innocent civilians died and a further 600 were wounded. By late afternoon, the revolt was suppressed, and Perón could broadcast a reassuring message. That might have been the end of it, but the evening brought unimagined horrors. Young men in trenchcoats looted and desecrated the cathedral, while others destroyed the headquarters of the archdiocese and burned down a dozen churches. These acts were totally unexpected; the sight of the ruined churches was a devastating blow to public morale and to the remains of Perón's reputation. He blamed communists and later even the Catholics; an official investigation implicated members of the Party but blamed the Masons. No one knows how far, if at all, the President was involved.

The next day, Perón repudiated the burning of the churches, ended the campaign against the Catholics and purged his cabinet. A month later, he announced that the Revolution was complete and welcomed opposition. Then, on 31 August, the papers announced that the President was going to resign. The CGT called a general strike and a huge crowd filled the Plaza to protest. They heard an astonishing speech: 'We will reply to violence with a greater violence . . . anyone in any place who tries to disturb the public order in opposition to the constituted authorities may be killed by any Argentine . . . when one of ours falls, five of theirs will'.[3] Perón withdrew his resignation. These words, which even alienated Peronists, sounded the alarm to the opposition. For the military, the last straw came on 7 September, when a delegation of the CGT offered to provide Perón with an armed workers' militia, as Eva had planned. Two generals, Pedro Aramburu and Eduardo Lonardi, took the lead against Perón, egged on by enthusiastic younger officers and the implacable navy.

The end came swiftly. On 16 September, the army at Cordoba broke into revolt, and the navy steamed from its bases toward the capital. By 19 September, loyalist forces were about to suppress the revolt when Perón unexpectedly transferred his authority to the army in what sounded like a resignation. Advances stopped and negotiations began. Perón, who had typically used ambiguous language, tried vainly to salvage his presidency, but the officers had accepted his resignation. With their agreement, Lonardi became provisional president and promised a constitutional government and free elections.

Perón's sudden collapse is a mystery. He had the means to defeat his foes, but apparently wanted to avoid bloodshed, as he had in 1943 and 1945; despite his bluster, Perón disliked violence and rarely resorted to force. Later, he claimed that he had been betrayed by the army and deserted by the workers. An immediate factor, which Perón took very seriously, was the navy's threat to blow up the refineries at La Plata, one of the great achievements of the regime. In any case, he went home on 20 September, packed a small bag with toilet articles and a picture of Eva and took refuge in the Paraguayan embassy. Lonardi made a triumphant entry into Buenos Aires, where enthusiastic crowds proclaimed the Liberating Revolution. Few of them ever expected to see Perón again.

The deposed dictator, waiting in a Paraguayan gunboat for permission to leave, wrote an affectionate letter to Nelly Rivas, signed 'Daddy' (it never reached her), while Dr Ara kept anxious vigil over his masterpiece, Eva's body.

EXILE, 1955–73

For seventeen years, Perón never set foot in Argentina, but his presence was still overwhelming. Despite the unrelenting hostility of the military, Perón maintained contact with his followers in the unions, who remained loyal to him and to the memory of Evita. His successful manipulation of them, and then of a new radical contingent, prevented the country from enjoying stability. During these years, Argentina had eight presidents, five of them generals. Democracy, sometimes preached, was never truly practised, for the military refused to allow any Peronist candidates. Finally, the last of the generals gave up the effort. The impossible happened: in 1973 the disgraced dictator was welcomed home by the largest crowd in Argentine history and freely elected as president in a landslide victory. But no one could have predicted that in September 1955.

Perón went to Paraguay, where he was warmly welcomed by his old friend President Stroessner; Perón promised him (quite falsely) that he would abstain from political activity. In November, pressure from Argentina forced Stroessner to send him on to Panama. Perón settled in Colón, where he became a familiar figure taking walks along the waterfront and attending boxing matches. He was also constantly corresponding with his followers at home and denouncing and hoping to undermine the government. In December an Argentine dance troupe, 'Joe Herald's Ballet' , variously described as folkloristic or a 'girlie show' visited Panama. One of its members was Maria Estela Martínez whom Perón met just before Christmas and soon installed as his secretary, then live-in girl friend. Isabel, as she was familiarly known, a petite and attractive 24-year-old, came from a middle-class background and had an elementary school education. She never left him, and was destined to make her own mark on Argentina.

The new Argentine regime under General Lonardi proclaimed 'neither victors nor vanquished', but moved swiftly against Perón's legacy. Congress and the Supreme Court were dissolved, leading Peronists arrested and Perón himself was stripped of his rank and the right to wear military uniform. In November, Lonardi succumbed to the first of the coups that were to plague the country. His successor, the hard-line General Aramburu, was determined to abolish all trace of Peronism. Military men took over the unions, the name of Perón disappeared from buildings, streets and towns, and all symbols of the Party were destroyed; mere possession of pictures of the hated tyrant or his wife could result in a jail sentence. The Eva Perón Foundation was dissolved and its name even cut out of the bedsheets it had provided.

Meanwhile, Evita's carefully embalmed body, reposing in the CGT headquarters, put the government in a quandary: for such loyal Catholics, cremation was out of the question, but burial could lead to demonstrations or the development of a cult. At the end of December 1955, the body was summarily removed to various sites (where it mysteriously attracted flowers and candles) until it wound up in a crate labelled 'radio parts' in the attic of an army building. The government soon decided it was too dangerous to keep in Argentina at all.

Aramburu took a fatal step in June 1956: he ordered the twenty-seven leaders of a revolt to be shot. Never in living memory had an Argentine government, not even Perón's, executed its opponents. The path of blood now opened ensured that the opposition would never be reconciled. The workers remained loyal to Perón, who appointed a leftist, John William Cooke, as his representative. Having escaped from Patagonian imprisonment, Cooke and other Party leaders were in constant touch with Perón, who typically only hinted at the policies he wanted followed, allowing him to take credit if they worked and shift the blame if they failed. His main policy was unremitting hostility to the military regime, expressed in sabotage and refusal to co-operate in the developing political process. It soon paid: in the elections of July 1957, the blank ballots of Perón's followers exceeded those of the other candidates. Politicians began to see the advantage of co-operating with the deposed leader.

The dead Evita no less than the living Juan was in the public eye. In November 1956, the government auctioned her jewels, which they claimed represented corruption and embezzlement. Works denouncing her as a resentful whore who dominated her weak husband began to appear, but so did evidence of a cult. Slum dwellers especially revered her memory and even set up informal shrines; for them, she was a saint. No one could honour her remains, though, for in early 1957, they were secretly buried in Italy. The precautions were so elaborate that not even Aramburu knew where the body rested.

Meanwhile, Perón's odyssey continued. In August 1956, he moved to another friendly dictatorship, Venezuela, where he continued to receive exiles and communicate with the home front. He lived simply in a country whose bitter contrasts of wealth and poverty disgusted him, but also in great danger, for the Argentine government made two attempts to assassinate him. His situation became more serious when the Venezuelan regime was overthrown in January 1957. Perón escaped to the Dominican Republic where the all-powerful Rafael Trujillo welcomed him. Trujillo gave him friendship, money and considerable freedom; they often met and dined together. During this peaceful interlude, Perón made a deal with the Radical party that enabled their leader Frondizi to be elected president in February 1958. He in turn proclaimed an amnesty for the Peronists, whom Perón still firmly controlled. After Fidel Castro's revolution of

January 1959, Perón replaced his radical representative Cooke with the more traditional union leader Augusto Vandor.

Perón made his final move in January 1960. Seeing that Trujillo's regime was in deep trouble, he settled in Spain, where he received a cool reception. Despite the memories of the Rainbow Tour, Franco had no love for Perón, whose attacks on the Church he resented; he tolerated but ignored him for thirteen years. The exile eventually settled in Madrid, living in the same building as Ava Gardner whose loud parties irritated him. By 1962, he started to build his own house in a comfortable suburb. He designed it, supervised the construction, named it the Seventeenth of October and delighted in its garden. During these years, Perón lived simply, with no sign of the stupendous wealth he was supposed to have stolen from Argentina: he had just enough to support himself and his entourage in comfort, and to maintain his contacts with his followers. Many of his expenses, as well as the cost of the house, were covered by the wealthy and devoted Jorge Antonio, who took charge of Perón's finances. Frondizi sent money after he was elected and by the 1960s the faithful unions at home were contributing $1,000 a month. But Perón never lived extravagantly and no trace of the rumoured Swiss accounts ever surfaced. His life became more respectable in November 1961, when he married Isabel, since Franco's Catholic regime did not countenance open cohabitation. She began to model herself on Evita, with her hair dyed blonde and pulled back.

Wherever he was, Perón was determined to return in triumph to Argentina. For the moment, that seemed a dim hope, but his interference in Argentine politics never flagged. His followers constantly appeared in Madrid, as did representatives of Frondizi, who allowed Peronists to contest local elections. When Perón's candidates were too successful, the military struck. They overthrew Frondizi in March 1962, introducing a confused and bitter time which Perón was quick to exploit. He first had to deal with his own men, notably Vandor, who was becoming too independent (there was even talk of him leading a 'Peronist without Perón' movement, an idea repugnant to the Leader). Perón set up a rival for him, following his usual tactic of keeping his friends as well as his enemies divided. A new election in July 1963 brought another civilian, Illia, to power, but with a feeble mandate since

Perón's blank ballots and allies actually got more votes.

This seemed the moment to move: Argentina had a weak government, constantly under attack from the unions guided by the puppet-master in Madrid, who was beginning to have serious health problems. Perhaps with this in mind, he announced his imminent return to Argentina. On 1 December, he was smuggled out of his villa in the boot of his car, and put on an Iberia flight bound for Buenos Aires via Rio. In Brazil, however, the authorities, who saw him as a source of trouble, detained him and put him on the next flight back to Spain. Many saw this humiliation as the end of Perón's political life.

In 1965, Perón celebrated his seventieth birthday; he had been away from Argentina for ten years. His life was regular and his health improved: he rose by 7 a.m., had a simple breakfast, took a walk, worked on his correspondence and fenced for an hour with Isabel (he never lost his love of sport) before lunch. After a siesta, he received visitors and sometimes went into town before dinner at 9 p.m. He then watched television or read until he went to bed at about midnight. He received a constant stream of visitors with the same unfailing courtesy he had always manifested. According to some, his reading gave him a more humane outlook, and the book he published in 1967, *Latinoamerica*, did propose a transfer of power to a younger generation. Yet at the same time, it was filled with crackpot notions of an 'international synarchy' of capitalists, communists, Masons, Zionists and Catholics to take over the world; the revolution that threw him out was supposedly one result. Yet this was nothing compared to the lunacy that accompanied a new figure, the most sinister of the whole period.

Since Perón could not reach Argentina himself, he started to use Isabel as his emissary. Despite her severe limitations of intellect and ability, she was his wife and could command respect; she was also no threat since she had no following of her own. During a nine-month stay in Argentina in 1965/6, when she helped to reassert Perón's authority over the movement, she met a former policeman and active astrologer, José López Rega. Among other accomplishments, he boasted that he had visited the stars and could raise the dead. He had published a thick book, co-written, he claimed, with the Archangel Gabriel. López Rega insinuated himself into Isabel's confidence, established an astonishing dominance over her and accompanied her on her return to Spain in May 1966. Perón, who was not charmed, threw him out, but was forced to bring him back after Isabel threatened to leave. He became Perón's private secretary and began to exercise an ever more disastrous influence.

Argentina, meanwhile, passed through a new crisis. After overthrowing the weak Illia regime on 28 June 1965, the military gave up on civilian rule and announced the Argentine Revolution, a military dictatorship intended to last for fifteen or twenty years. Perón and his followers accommodated themselves to the new leader, General Onganía, who tolerated their activities. The popularity of the new regime, however, faded as it became apparent that Onganía was an ultra-conservative moralist whose anger fell first on miniskirts, then, more seriously, on the left. By 1968, Perón was urging his followers not to co-operate with the government, while at the same time making sure that their divided leadership proved no threat to him. In spite of that, the regime seemed unshakeable until a disaster that ushered in a decade of violent instability.

In May 1969, the industrial city of Córdoba broke into revolt. The trouble started with student unrest, soon spread to the workers and required massive military intervention to suppress. It caused extensive damage to the city and the regime, and the violence spread. On 2 June, fifteen US-owned supermarkets were firebombed, and on the 30th Vandor was assassinated; the crime was never solved. Robberies, kidnappings and attacks on the military spread throughout the country. They culminated on the anniversary of the Córdoba uprising, when ex-President Aramburu was kidnapped and murdered by a previously unknown group, the Montoneros. This event, which horrified the nation, marked the end for Onganía. On 8 June, he was replaced by a military junta, which had to deal with the mounting chaos.

One of the demands the Montoneros had made on Aramburu was the return of Eva's body. By now, she had become the heroine of the radical left who adored her last violent speeches, saw her as a link with the people and claimed to be acting like her when they took from the rich and gave to the poor. The Montoneros, who started as a band of twelve middle-class Catholic youths, were one of several extremist organizations. The most intransigent was the People's Revolutionary Army (ERP) which remained Marxist. The FAR (Revolutionary Armed Forces), founded to support Che Guevara, gradually swung toward Perón, whose attitude was highly ambiguous. He never disavowed the terrorists, whom he swiftly recognized as a valuable means of attacking the government and of balancing his working-class followers. They implausibly saw him as a revolutionary, partly because of their image of Evita, partly because he was the prime anti-establishment figure, hated by all governments since their childhood and partly, perhaps, because they had spent their earliest years subjected to the constant propaganda of Peronism. Their idealism exceeded their reason, for there was nothing in Perón's record (as opposed to his words) that would comfort a revolutionary.

The next coup, in March 1971, brought forward General Alejandro Lanusse, a well-connected former prisoner of Perón. More realistic than any of his predecessors, he recognized that the only hope of stability lay in accepting the reality of Perón and Peronism. Within a month, he lifted the ban on the Peronists, hoping that he could bring their leader into the open and tie him down to concrete policies that might undermine his support. He sadly

tried to put it to practical use: lighting candles beside the coffin, he had Isabel lie on top while he chanted phrases designed to lift Eva's spiritual essence into her unworthy successor. His efforts failed. As for Perón, he was far less concerned with Eva's memory than were many of his followers.

Perón's mind was focused on his own return to power. He had never wavered from his goal, which started to seem more realistic when Lanusse announced elections for March 1973. Perón appointed the obsequious Hector Cámpora as his representative in Argentina; Cámpora in turn allowed only one candidate for each post in the legalized Justicialist Party, guaranteeing Perón's supreme control. The left welcomed Cámpora, not noticing that Perón had appointed a hard-line rightist, Colonel Osinde, as his personal adviser. They also rationalized Perón's alliance with Frondizi and other non-revolutionary parties. Outwardly, Perón still espoused revolutionary causes, justifying leftist violence as a response to an oppressive government. He realized the tactical value of the left and never doubted that he could ultimately control it. As he said before the elections, 'the left is like the vinegar in the salad; you have to put a little in so you can eat it'.[2]

He did nothing to stop the terrorists, who marked the twentieth anniversary of Eva's death with twenty time bombs that exploded simultaneously in targets associated with the Oligarchy.

None of this stopped Perón from returning to Argentina for the first time in seventeen years on 17 November 1972. He took up residence in a suburban house where throngs came to acclaim the famous elder statesman. Perón had not lost his popular touch: he stood regularly on his balcony to greet the welcoming crowds, but also carried on serious political business. A pact with Frondizi produced a coalition which proceeded to nominate Perón. He declined, then, to great astonishment, appointed the servile Cámpora as candidate, to be an interim office holder who could take the blame if anything went wrong or, if not, lay the foundation for the Leader's return. Perón returned to Madrid. The faithful duly supported Cámpora, but the new election slogan 'Cámpora to government, Perón to power' left no doubt where their loyalties lay.

Although Cámpora fell a fraction short of a majority in the election, everyone including his opponent the radical Balbín agreed that he should assume office. His inauguration on 25 May 1973 was a triumph, with a huge crowd of 500,000, carefully monitored by the radical youth organizations, who allowed only presidents Allende of Chile and Dorticós of Cuba to pass through. Radical shouts of 'Socialist fatherland' were answered by labour's 'Peronist Fatherland', but there was no serious violence. Perón himself stayed away. Cámpora's new cabinet ominously included López Rega, who went to Eva's old base, the Ministry of Social Welfare. The new President announced plans to reopen the Foundation, and had Eva's office refurbished. In general, his policies envisaged a greater role for the state, and were favorable to the left.

Perón's activities also seemed to suggest a swerve to the left. After making a mysterious trip to Romania in February (perhaps to get rejuvenation treatments), he sent Isabel and López Rega to China and North Korea. But he soon showed his true colours by summoning the Peronist youth leaders to Madrid; he wanted to bring them under his firm control and to isolate the Marxist ERP. None of this stopped the violence at home, especially since Cámpora's interior minister announced that the government would not repress what he called the people's initiatives. The confusion suited Perón, for it was obvious to everyone that he alone could bring a solution. On 19 June, therefore, Franco bade farewell to Perón, his first and last contact with his long-term guest. The Madrid household was packed up, and the exile started home.

EIGHT

RETURN AND LEGACY, 1973–89

On 20 June 1973, a million and a half people, the greatest crowd in the history of Argentina, assembled at Perón's Ezeiza airport to greet their now beloved leader and best hope. What should have been the most glorious occasion of Perón's career turned into an ominous disaster. Government forces occupied the area around the platform where Perón was to speak, but the left soon arrived in force and someone started firing. Right and left shot at each other, the crowd stampeded and hundreds were killed. Perón received the news as his plane was approaching Argentina. To his disgust, it had to be diverted to a military airfield and the party brought in quietly to the presidential residence, where Perón gave a reassuring broadcast.

The next day Perón addressed the public on law and order, discipline and work. His words held no comfort for the left. The next day he met Balbín, with whom he had established surprisingly friendly relations, and agreed a policy of political co-operation. On 11 June, Cámpora restored Perón's military rank, and two days later resigned office, an action that caused some surprise. It seems clear, though, that Perón never envisaged Cámpora as more than an interim figurehead and that he planned to take over direct rule as soon as the dust had settled. His constantly deteriorating health may have been a factor; Perón may also have wanted to assume power while he could still function,

The new election was scheduled for 23 September. The presidential nomination was never in doubt, but the post of vice-president was extremely important because of Perón's age and health. A rumoured Perón–Balbín coalition might have pleased everyone, but the Party nominated Isabel. This irrational choice astonished the Peronist youth and much of the public. It was also filled with irony since a Perón–Perón ticket was Eva's frustrated hope in 1951. Then, the army blocked it; now everyone fell in line behind the Leader's choice. Perón had eliminated virtually everybody in his party who displayed leadership qualities, and knew that Isabel, not identified with right or left, could be counted on to carry out his will.

The march that the CGT mobilized in support of the candidates on 31 August was a great success. A million workers paraded past Perón, who showed his stamina by remaining on the balcony of the Union headquarters for eight hours. The election seemed only an aftermath. Perón's triumphant 62 per cent of the vote represented a broad cross-section of society. His years of waiting had finally paid off.

On 12 October 1973, Perón, standing on the balcony of the Casa Rosada and wearing his general's uniform for the first time in eighteen years, was inaugurated for his third term as president. He had achieved the impossible: the once reviled dictator was now freely elected with a broad mandate. He had to deal with an economy ravaged by inflation, but the more immediate problems were political: how to reconcile right and left, how to suppress terrorism and restore the civil society he had done so much to undermine. Perón had the method but not the means; as he told Frondizi, he could end the violence if he were a dictator, but he was too old for that. At seventy-eight and in failing health, he realized that his time and energies were limited.

The radical youth fondly imagined that the Perón they had loyally supported was their man. Far from it, he made their nemesis, López Rega, his intermediary, then announced a typical Peronist solution: all the youth organizations should combine into a grand confederation which the government would control. The Marxist ERP, which never accepted Perón, would have nothing to do with it, and the Peronist youth were reluctant. In response, Perón allowed the right-wing militants of López Rega a free hand. Since the ERP had gone underground, the brunt of the attacks fell on the Peronist radicals. Left-leaning governors were replaced and radicals purged from the local administrations. He left no doubt that he would not tolerate any group, however friendly, that was not completely submissive.

These political problems prevented Perón from achieving much on other fronts. A large-scale trade agreement with Cuba, defying the American embargo, and a law that gave the universities a surprising degree of autonomy – essentially turning them over to the left – were among his few accomplishments. None of this assuaged the radicals whose violence continued. The new regime avoided many of the excesses of the old. No streets or towns were named for Perón or Evita, though López Rega did pursue a favourite project, the Altar of the Fatherland. This was to be a grandiose monument, celebrating Argentine history and containing the mortal remains of Evita.

Perón himself still had his old charm and some energy, especially in the mornings, but his health gave little hope for a long or successful administration. A week after his return, he had a heart attack, which was kept secret, and in November barely escaped death when his lungs filled with liquid. Nevertheless, the President kept up his activities and made plans for the future.

At his inauguration, Perón had promised to reappear on May Day to hear the opinion of the public. It was a bitter disappointment. Though the workers were friendly, half the crowd consisted of young radicals who let their Leader know what they thought. They jeered the traditional crowning of a beauty queen, shouted 'there is only one Evita' when Isabel appeared and engaged in a hostile dialogue with Perón, who lost his temper and substituted a string of insults for the rest of his speech. The youths turned their backs on him and marched away to the jeers and attacks of the workers. Perón's manipulation of the left had come back to haunt him.

On 12 June, Perón made what was to be his last public appearance. He sounded as if he were giving a final blessing to the assembled workers. A few days later, he caught a cold which turned into pneumonia. Isabel and López Rega were summoned from their missions in Europe to attend the Conductor who expired shortly after dawn on 1 July 1974. Perón had had no children. His third term had lasted less than eight months. Although there was a massive outpouring of genuine feeling for a figure who had been loved or hated, but never out of the public eye, for thirty years, the funeral was simple and the body was not embalmed, in accordance with Perón's own orders. He left the presidency to Isabel who would try in vain to justify the name and position she held.

The new President made it clear that she intended to keep López Rega as her chief adviser. He remained dominant, even to the extent of mouthing her speeches as she spoke because, he claimed, the words came through him from Perón in the spirit world. Neither spirits nor these two humans, though, could stem the flood of problems. As long as Perón had been alive, there might be some hope of reconciliation or stability. Now, the guerrillas broke into open revolt, to be faced with the death squads of López Rega. In October, the Montoneros struck. They stole the body of ex-President Aramburu from his tomb, announcing they would only return it when Evita's was brought back to Argentina. On 17 November 1974, her remains finally returned from Madrid where Perón had left them. They were installed temporarily in the presidential residence, next to her husband's remains, awaiting completion of the Altar of the Fatherland.

Neither of the dead Peróns could save the living one. López Rega was the first to go. After a demonstration in July when workers for the first time marched against a Peronist government, he left the country. Isabel's turn came on 25 March 1976. She was deposed and put under house arrest, finally returning to Spain in 1981. Another junta took over, more ferocious than any before. To deal with terrorism, the military embarked on a savage campaign of repression. Judicial formalities were ignored as real and supposed subversives were rounded up, tortured and slaughtered. At the cost of some 9,000 lives, Argentina solved the problem of terrorism. By the end of 1977, the Montoneros and other radicals were nowhere in sight. Nor was Peronism or the Peróns. The new leader, General Videla, had refused to move into the presidential residence as long as the bodies were there. Perón was buried in his family's plot and Evita, finally, on 22 October 1976, was laid to rest, ironically in the most aristocratic of Buenos Aires' cemeteries, beside her devoted brother Juan. A special steel-lined chamber, proof against even atomic attack, sheltered her remains and made them totally inaccessible.

The military presided over a declining economy until 1982 when its defeat in the Falkland War led to elections that restored democracy. Despite everything, Peronism was still alive. The workers had not forgotten their champion and huge numbers still cherished the memory of Evita's personal touch. The Party revived and grew as Argentina's problems festered until, in 1989, a Peronist president, Carlos Menem, once again occupied the Casa Rosada. Ten years later, he was still in office, and the images of Juan and Evita, the eternal symbols of their party, were once again displayed in public.

Argentina felt the presence of Juan Perón as none other in modern history. He was constantly in power or in the public eye for thirty years, and twenty years after his death was still a powerful symbol. Evita's star shone more briefly, but more brilliantly, and left a glow that has never faded. If people can be objective about Perón, they can only love or hate Evita. Together, they shifted the country on to a new course: the common people were treated with a new respect and brought fully into the workings of the country, women were integrated into political life and social welfare became an essential part of the government's activities. Perón did not kill his enemies.

Yet, the balance sheet remains negative. Perón strove to create a rich, powerful, modern Argentina that would have great influence in South America and the wider world. Instead, he left its economy in a shambles, allowed violent political dissension to threaten its very fabric and lived to see it fall far behind its great rival Brazil. Perón's self-advancement and disdain for others led him to crush anyone with ability and surround himself with incompetents. His flirtation with the radicals to advance his own cause encouraged endless violence.

His determination to return made Argentina ungovernable at a crucial time and left a legacy of instability that has only in recent times been resolved. While she was alive, Evita maintained a liaison with the people and restrained Perón's erratic behavior. With her, Perón's rule enjoyed some real success; without her, it faded into failure, despite its real accomplishments.

NOTES

CHAPTER 2

1. N. Fraser and M. Navarro, *Eva Perón*, New York, Norton, 1980, p. 22.
2. A. Dujovne Ortiz, *Eva Perón*, London, Warner, 1997, p. 52.

CHAPTER 3

1. J. Page, *Perón*, New York, Random House, 1983, p. 112; *Time*, 12 June 1944.

CHAPTER 4

1. Page, *Perón*, p. 161.
2. Fraser and Navarro, *Eva Perón*, p. 82.

CHAPTER 5

1. Page, *Perón*, p. 235.
2. G. Blanksten, *Perón's Argentina*, University of Chicago, 1953, p. 118.
3. J. Barnes, *Evita – First Lady*, New York, Grove, 1978, p. 80.
4. E. Perón, *Discursos Completos*, 2 vols, Buenos Aires, Megafón, 1985, pp. 353–5, partly quoted by Fraser and Navarro, *Eva Perón*, p. 146.

CHAPTER 6

1. Perón, *Discursos Completos*, Vol. 2, pp. 415–17, partly translated in Page, *Perón*, p. 258.
2. Page, *Perón*, p. 300.
3. Page, *Perón*, p. 315.

Notes

CHAPTER 7

1. Page, *Perón*, p. 420.
2. R. Crassweller, *Perón and the Enigma of Argentina*, New York, Norton, 1987, p. 350.

BIBLIOGRAPHY

The best biographies of the Peróns are:

Fraser, Nicholas and Navarro, Marysa. *Eva Perón*, London, André Deutsch and New York, Norton, 1980
Page, Joseph. *Perón*, New York, Random House, 1983

The following are also useful:

Alexander, Robert. *Juan Domingo Perón: A History*, Boulder, Westview, 1979
Barnes, John. *Evita – First Lady*, New York, Grove, 1978
Blanksten, George. *Perón's Argentina*, University of Chicago, 1953 (analysis of government)
Crassweller, Robert. *Perón and the Enigma of Argentina*, New York, Norton, 1987 (good for background)
Cowles, Fleur. *Bloody Precedent*, New York, Random House, 1952 (very negative)
de Elia, Tomás and Queiroz, Juan Pablo. *Evita, an Intimate Portrait of Eva Perón*, New York, Rizzoli, 1997 (superb photographs)
Main, Mary. *Evita, The Woman With the Whip*, London, Corgi, 1977 (classic negative version)
Ortiz, Alicia Dujovne. *Eva Perón*, London, Warner, 1997 (novelistic)

Bibliography

Page, Joseph (ed.). *In My Own Words, Evita*, New York, New Press, 1996

Perón, Eva. *Discursos Completos*, 2 vols, Buenos Aires, Megafón, 1985 (speeches)

———. *Evita by Evita*, London, Proteus, 1978 (ghost-written autobiography)

Perón, Juan. *Yo, Juan Domingo Perón*, Barcelona, Planeta, 1976 (memoirs)

Taylor, J.A. *Eva Perón, The Myths of a Woman*, University of Chicago, 1979

POCKET BIOGRAPHIES

AVAILABLE

Beethoven
Anne Pimlott Baker

Ellen Terry
Moira Shearer

Mao Zedong
Delia Davin

David Livingstone
C.S. Nicholls

Scott of the Antarctic
Michael De-la-Noy

Abraham Lincoln
H.G. Pitt

Alexander the Great
E.E. Rice

Marie and Pierre Curie
John Senior

Sigmund Freud
Stephen Wilson

Margot Fonteyn
Alastair Macaulay

Marilyn Monroe
Sheridan Morley and
Ruth Leon

Enid Blyton
George Greenfield

Rasputin
Harold Shukman

Winston Churchill
Robert Blake

Jane Austen
Helen Lefroy

George IV
Michael De-la-Noy

For a copy of our complete list or details of other Sutton titles, please contact Emma Leitch at Sutton Publishing Limited, Phoenix Mill, Thrupp, Stroud, Gloucestershire, GL5 2BU